Chuck Sturm

how successful
leaders
bounce
back
from
setbacks

THE
Adversity
Challenge

Charles R. Stoner
John F. Gilligan

For permission requests, contact the publisher at:

Executive Excellence Publishing
1366 East 1120 South
Provo, UT 84606
Phone: 1-801-375-4060
Toll Free: 1-800-304-9782
Fax: 1-801-377-5960
www.eep.com

For Executive Excellence books, magazines, and other products, contact Executive Excellence directly. Call 1-800-304-9782, fax 1-801-377-5960, or visit our Website at www.eep.com.

eep.com

Printed in the United States

10 9 8 7 6 5 4 3 2 1

Library of Congress Catalog-in-Publication Data

Stoner, Charles R., Gilligan John F.
   The adversity challenge : how successful leaders bounce back from setbacks / Charles R. Stoner, John F. Gilligan.
      p. cm.
Includes bibliographical references.
   ISBN 1-930771-16-9
   HD49 .S76 2001
   658.4/092 21
                        2001004877

Advance Praise for

The Adversity Challenge

"This is a timely book for those who have a leadership role in today's turbulent economy. It comments and draws conclusions from in-depth interviews with seasoned executives. The book demonstrates how successful leaders bounce back from the depths of adversity and lead their companies to success. It is a unique book that is a must read for those who would survive and prosper in the years ahead."

—Gerald D. Stephens, CPCU Chairman RLI Corp.

"This is a book about courage: the courage to bounce back again and again, often in the face of trying odds. Its message, drawn from the personal stories of successful leaders, is critical for anyone facing the challenges of today's turbulent business setting."

—Max De Pree, author of *Leadership Jazz*

"This book is well done. It captures the essence of several individuals' unique personal experiences and presents them as living principles in a way that every reader can understand and relate to their own situation."

—Everett Alvarez Jr., Commander USN, retired; POW 1964 to 1973

"*The Adversity Challenge* concisely articulates the life process most business leaders experience that has helped qualify them for their current responsibility. *The Adversity Challenge* will help many of us understand what we have or are experiencing and how to best leverage our situation for the good of our companies."

—William D. Morton, Chairman and CEO, Morton Industrial Group, Inc.

"Adversity is a reality of life. Chuck Stoner and Jack Gilligan help us understand how it can shape and mold the leader and how it can be overcome and used by the leader to provide positive direction for those being led."
　　　　—C. William Pollard, Chairman, The ServiceMaster Company

"Drawing from the experiences of successful leaders, the authors offer practical and sound advice for dealing with the trials and tribulations of business and life. This is an important book for both new and seasoned leaders, and also for the general public."
　　　　—U.S. Congressman Ray LaHood

"Successful leaders have the amazing capacity to quickly and dramatically respond to adversity. This book could not be more timely, given the leadership that followed the profound adversity that struck the U.S.A. on September 11, 2001."
　　　　—George A. Schaefer, Chairman of the Board,
　　　　retired, Caterpillar, Inc.

"This book is a must read for every leader and those who work with leaders. Understanding adversity and its role in the leadership journey is essential. Every leader knows that adversity goes with the choice to lead. This book will guide leaders through the process of transformation necessary to achieve greatness."
　　　　—John Izzo, Ph.D., author of *Awakening Corporate Soul* and *Values Shift*

ACKNOWLEDGMENTS

We wish to thank the following participants in this study for the generosity of their time in granting us a personal interview about their leadership career. More importantly, we thank them for their insights, openness, and candor in sharing their personal struggles as well as their success in their professional journey.

Bashir Ali, Workforce Development Director, City of Peoria
Bruce L. Alkire, Executive Vice President, The Finch Companies
Mary A. Ardapple, President, Apple's Bakery, Inc.
Michael D. Bailie, M.D., Vice Dean, University of Illinois College of Medicine
William R. Barrick, Retired Partner, KPMG Peat Marwick
Dick Blaudow, President/CEO, ATS
Tom Bower, President, Bower Communications
Robert W. Brown, President, CEO, and Chair, BankPlus
Laraine Bryson, President, Urban League
John Brazil, Ph.D., President, Trinity University
Larry Clore, President, Multi-Ad Services, Inc.
A. Wayne Flittner, Former CEO and Chairman, Ross Advertising, Inc.
Diana J. Hall, President, Bard Optical
Roger T. Kelley, Founder, The Leadership Development Center
Robert Klaus, President, Klaus Companies
Michel McCord, CEO, Illinois Mutual Life Insurance Company
Robert A. McCord, Chairman Emeritus, Illinois Mutual Life Insurance Company
Michael D. McKnight, City Manger, City of Peoria
William D. Morton, Chairman and CEO, Morton Industrial Group, Inc.
Diane Oberhelman, President, Cullinan Properties, LTD
Nick Owens, Chairman and CEO, Hagerty Brothers Company
David P. Ransburg, Chairman and CEO, L.R. Nelson Corporation
Jack Russell, Assistant Director, The Leadership Development Center
John G. Sahn, Adminstrator/CEO, John C. Proctor Endowment
George A. Schaefer, Chairman of the Board, Retired, Caterpillar, Inc.
John Stenson, Superintendent of Police, City of Peoria
Gerald D. Stephens, Chairman of the Board, Founder, RLI Corp.
Thomas E. Spurgeon, President and CEO, Lincoln Office
Thomas Thomas, President Emeritus, Illinois Central College
Jay R. Vonachen, President, Vonachen Service & Supply
Charles E. Weaver, President, Weaver Enterprises
Robert Viets, Retired President and CEO, CILCORP, Inc.
Glenn A. Werry, Jr., President/CEO, Star Transport, Inc.
Mary Cay Westphal, President/Owner, Shamrock Plastics
Michael R. Wiesehan, Vice President, Lippmann's Furniture & Interiors, Inc.

Contents

Part V: The Path Through Adversity—Insight

Part VI: The Path Through Adversity—Transformation

Part VII: The Lessons of Experience

Preface

This book is built upon the proposition that successful leaders are forged in the crucible of adversity. We discover what each of us senses and knows intuitively: The road to success is a jagged and twisting path. It includes profound peaks and hellish valleys that can be consuming and overwhelming, or challenging and transformational. No one escapes. All must ride through the valleys. While each valley may differ, the process of passing through them does not.

That process was revealed and validated by research and in-depth interviews with 35 successful business leaders. By and large, these leaders came from smaller and mid-sized businesses. They are the men and women who exemplify business leadership. Most are not the champions of major organizations whose stories are carried in the *Wall Street Journal*. They represent the other 99.9 percent of business leaders who struggle and succeed and who are the backbone of industry. In the following pages, you will learn of their stories, and you will read their words.

Following the major proposition that successful leaders are forged in the crucible of adversity, we explore how successful leaders bounce back or rebound from their adversities. This is the core of the book. Beginning with the adverse event called the "Great Disruption," we trace the successful leader's journey through three phases: *Disillusionment, Reflection,* and *Adaptation*. This is **the rebound process.**

We attempt to go beyond merely describing the journey, which, at times, seems more like a roller coaster. Knowing about something and knowing what to do about it are two different, albeit related, realities. While it is certainly important to understand the process of what happens when confronted with a Great Disruption, it is more important to know how to respond to it. This is what we disclose, based upon what successful leaders have actually done in these circumstances. In the end, we hope that the wisdom of their experiences will assist you in becoming a more effective leader.

The early chapters deal directly with leadership and success, and the final chapters provide sound advice on preparing you to face your own adversities. Our intent is to offer an opportunity for you to learn from others who have made a successful journey through adversity. And having done so, it is our hope that you may find yourself properly forewarned and therefore forearmed.

Chuck Stoner and Jack Gilligan, Peoria, Illinois
January 2002

Introduction

The book is divided into seven parts.

Part I focuses on leadership and success. The essence of leadership is explored as is the meaning of success. This is done within the context of adversity and the critical role it plays in forming leadership and in defining success.

Part II addresses the nature of adversity. Here we will examine the arena of adversity and look carefully at the tests of adversity. You will recognize the hurdles and in all likelihood, be able to identify with the struggles we unfold. Importantly, we detail the adversity cycle—the process through which adversity transforms leaders.

Part III addresses the support networks that successful leaders turn to when facing adversity. We will explore the role of family, friends, colleagues, and spirituality as they serve as important support networks. You will see the critical roles played by these networks, and how they are used within the framework of adversity and crisis.

Part IV addresses the great disruption of adversity. Here, we explain how the adversity events affect leaders and their course of progress and success.

Part V deals directly with the first phase of the leader rebound: insight. This includes the nature of disillusionment and reflection as a function of the great disruption in the life of the leader. The specific actions that make the leader rebound possible are identified.

Part VI continues the exploration of the leader rebound. Its focus is on the rebound transformation. We argue that a proper adjustment to adversity brings about a transformation in the leader that makes for a better leader and person. Not all succeed in this process.

Part VII addresses the lessons of adversity. Here we discuss what leaders learn and what they become as a result of their rebound transformation. Further, we explore how these lessons from adversity are transferred to others and how they may enhance organizational life. Furthermore, we will discuss how leaders transfer their rebound attitude and approach to their organizations.

There is a difference between having knowledge and gaining wisdom. One can possess information and knowledge without wisdom. Wisdom is about the right use and application of knowledge and information based on the insights of experience.

At the end of each chapter we will conclude with a section entitled *The Wisdom of Experience*, which captures the key insights that flow from the chapter. In short, you will see the leader rebound emerge, piece by piece, as we move through the book. These are succinct capsules that highlight the most important themes stressed in the chapter. They are good to keep in mind. They also offer a quick review as you move to the next chapter, and they serve as a foundation as you move to the next level of the leader rebound.

Our intent is to provide a work that is both thoughtful and practical. We are convinced you will find *The Adversity Challenge* to be an interesting journey. We're also convinced that it will make sense and hold great relevance to you as you move along your personal leadership journey.

PART
I

LEADERSHIP
AND SUCCESS

1

The Leader's Journey:
Looking at the Unworn Path to Success

"The old adage—adversity builds character—is simply a fact."

Norman Brinker, the restaurant magnate whose holdings included Chili's and Macaroni Grill, was a role model of leader success. An innovator and a true pioneer, Brinker is credited with defining the casual dining segment of the restaurant industry. As an avid sportsman and polo enthusiast, Brinker regularly played polo. During a match in 1993, Brinker suffered a near fatal injury when he was broadsided at full speed by a galloping horse.

Defying the odds and the opinions of his doctors, Brinker returned to work only months after the accident. Addressing his staff on the day of his emotional return, Brinker noted, "Negative thinking is the first step backward, and that means no progress. I was more excited about the good things that were happening. I wasn't depressed about the negative side of things."[1]

I met Norman three years later and had a chance to spend some time with him. His spirit amazed me. I knew he still went through a rigorous and demanding regimen of recovery that included intense therapy sessions. I realized that walking, even a relatively short distance, was painful for him. Yet he demonstrated a remarkable resiliency and a wonderful attitude. He seemed to accept this life event, this crisis, as another challenge—a challenge that he approached with persistence and commitment to overcome. Somehow, there was solution and resolve. He displayed the leader rebound.

This project began as a book about success. But it grew into much more as the 35 leaders interviewed candidly revealed a side of their careers and lives rarely laid before the public. Their stories were deeply personal. At times, they were surprising. They drove to the core, the very essence, of the executive life. They presented stories of amazing achievements and dramatic mistakes. They openly admitted a frequent contrast between their cool public demeanor and their inner struggle with the mixed emotions of uncertainty. They spoke of how family, friends, mentors, and personal spirituality had affected their quest for success. They spoke of choices and tradeoffs in their careers and lives. Throughout, one theme remained constant: Courage, the courage to respond and come back again and again, often in the face of damning odds. We found it impossible to ignore the intensity of this theme. This is their story.

The interviews were very personal and self-disclosing. We want to respect the confidentiality of what was revealed during these conversations. Consequently, we have not identified any of those in our study with their words and life events. Their words and life events speak for themselves and illustrate the major findings and themes in this book. Since there is no need to identify persons, we have not done so.

An Unexpected Encounter

It was a spacious corner office, and the nameplate simply read: "President and CEO." The walls were filled with photos of dignitaries, hands clasped, and smiling faces. I recognized a politician, a sports hero, and an industry honcho. There were carefully pruned and laminated newspaper and magazine items heralding the achievements of the business. Clearly, this was a man of power and accomplishment. I'd worked for the CEO's company as a consultant on a few occasions and had exchanged pleasantries with him over the years. I realized that these contacts were probably the main reason I was able to capture some of his time, especially when it was clear that this was an academic exploration of leader success.

I was thrown off stride from the start. With proper academic focus, we had developed a careful interviewing outline. I initiated the protocol, but he quickly intervened. "To understand me and my career, you really have to know something more about me, about my past, what I've experienced, and where I've come from."

Dramatically, he returned to his childhood. He spoke of his father—a man of character. Spanning back over for 40 years, he spoke with intensity, passion, and clarity, as if the events had just transpired. He spoke of admiration, and while the term was never used, he spoke of love. He also spoke of death. There was a strange humility and emotion as he recounted his father's unexpected illness and untimely death. He admitted his deep loss, confusion, search, and growth as he struggled to first exist and then move on.

Of all the things in his life and in his organizational career, why share this? This painful experience was etched so profoundly into his character that he felt he could not define himself and his success without returning to this story. Why? Something happened there. Life shaping had occurred in the depths of adversity. Devastation and despair had been met, and those demons had not won. The lesson was one of resilience; a lesson that he repeated over and again, although the context would change. He saw it when his first business had to be sold, when his career path was in crisis, and when his own personal health began to unravel.

Then he talked about coming back. He spoke with a fervor and fire more characteristic of an evangelist than a business leader. Perhaps sensing my confusion, he offered an interpretation: "What are these experiences about? This is where we find ourselves. This is where we find out if we're any good. This is where we start to find out that there's rich meaning in all the seemingly negative things that happen to us. I didn't climb the mountain successfully the first time. So I'm going to reorganize, go back, and climb it again."

The Inevitability of Adversity

We live with a myth. It goes something like this: You can do and be anything you set your mind to do and be. If you put your nose to the grindstone, work hard, move with dedication and persistence, and provide the proper dose of hard work, you will achieve your goals. You will be successful.

This myth has been promoted throughout our schools and encouraged by the media. We pass it to our children and encourage them to take it to heart. We engrain it into our organizational systems. It is not a bad myth. In fact, it is a myth that fosters hard work, enthusiasm, and has undoubtedly helped produce many of the most prominent achievements of our age. Yet, it is still a myth. It argues a linear progression to success. It promotes an expectation that if things are done properly and executed correctly, then success will result.

The proposition is too simplistic. It misses the mark, not in its good counsel, but in its inconsistency with the real world and real living. This linear view of success provides a wonderful platitude, but it is a confusing guide for the reality of the world.

The linear model of thinking assumes that successful leaders should prevent adversities and crises. In fact, the model asserts that if proper consideration, planning, and reading of the situation occurs, then a crisis should be, for all practical purposes, avoidable.

Of course, each of us understands reality. We recognize the fallacy and limitation of the linear model. The trouble is that most of us, in the midst of activity, fail to accept that life and leadership are not linear. One of the characteristics we saw in our leaders was a clear understanding and acceptance of the nonlinear nature of life. They seemed to recognize that adversities will arise, problems will emerge, and breakdowns will pop up. Random events occur.

While careful planning and execution may minimize the occurrence or impact, randomness is a fact of organizational life—of life itself—and confronting adversity because of this is inevitable. Importantly, these leaders did not self destruct, instead they moved on. In fact, it was in the random, crisis phases of life that their leadership was forged.

If leadership is not a path of continual, incremental positive moves that collectively add to success, what is it? Leadership is about many things, but it always includes a series of ups and downs, wins and losses, which when taken in aggregate, spell success. Leaders, like the previously mentioned executive, realize that their lives are made of peaks and valleys. Further, they understand that while the peaks are exciting, the most profound growth occurs in the valleys. In some strange and complicated way, adversity becomes a transforming experience.

The Leader Rebound

One of our interviewees, a CEO of a rapidly expanding mid-sized business, said it best: "No matter how difficult a challenge, there's a way to overcome it. Do I get down? Absolutely. Do I get frustrated and upset? Absolutely. But once I get over that I say,

'Okay, there's got to be a way to deal with this.' I think the best things happen when some crisis or disaster challenges us."

Some face adversity and rise and succeed. Some do not. What makes the difference? Is it just good psychological health or personality? If something happens during adversity, what is it? And if some experience the power of positive transformation, how does it occur? We probed during our interviews to find guidance and direction. Some leaders gave a clear personal prescription. Others recognized the ability to keep coming back but had difficulty in providing a form or structure for their behavior.

In attempting to understand and categorize, we turned to the literature and prevailing research to draw patterns that explain how to approach and handle adversities, hardships, and crises. The Norman Brinkers of this world are able to reframe crisis into a challenge and harness their resolve to move on. This never happens suddenly or magically. So how does it occur? The answers are not simple. But it is those answers, that leader rebound, which we explore in this book.

2

Leadership

"The village idiot can lead when everything's going along great. It's when things aren't so great that we really show our leadership."

He is a seasoned executive. He has served as president for two different manufacturing companies. He loves his work and is presently the CEO of a third business. With over 30 years of executive experience, his perspective is broad.

There have been good times and bad. Out of it all, he knows through the pleasure and pain of experience that success ultimately depends upon people who work for him. He has learned that his greatest resource is indeed the human resource. Experience has demonstrated that nothing ever gets accomplished without the collaboration and cooperation of both management and labor. For him, knowing how to do this is the fundamental role of leadership. Like many executives of his stature, he has served and continues to serve on the boards of many community and not-for-profit organizations. A tough, experienced, no-holds-barred straight shooter, he is an opinionated and respected leader. By all obvious measures, he is a success.

He has never led a Fortune 500 company. You'd probably not read about him in the national business press. His businesses are mid-sized firms employing hundreds—not hundreds of thousands—of people. In most cases, he knows his people. He is visible and unbuffered by layers of bureaucracy. He is the face and image of management to the people of his organizations.

Most of you work in organizations like those he has led. Most of you work with executives like him. These executives are people a lot like you, from companies a lot like yours. We are convinced that their insights will make sense to you.

They talk about success, failure, business, and family. They speak of roadblocks and challenges, achievements and mistakes. Importantly, they speak openly about adversities, those real tests of character that are part and parcel of executive life. Their message is frank, uplifting, and encouraging—it is real. Their insights and suggestions speak to emerging leaders as well as seasoned leaders. Their message is a wonderful statement for all who are assuming and struggling with the mantle of leadership.

The Mantle of Leadership[1]

In recent years, the world of leadership has come under fire. There is probably some logic to the criticism. Many of the stories carried in daily newspapers and magazines raise concerns about the state and condition of leadership. Examples of leaders bending standards pepper the news. Headline-grabbing stories of leaders moving in morally questionable territory seize our attention. Cynics argue that we are facing a dearth of leadership.

While problems certainly do exist, these cynics present, at best, a partial picture. The landscape of business is changing rapidly. Organizational demands are pressing and are at times chaotic. Each day brings new decisions and new challenges, each fraught with peril and risk.

Leaders must have the courage to assess situations, weigh the risks, consider options, and then act. Of course, the need for quick thinking and action must be balanced against the need for careful strategic analysis. The need for continual innovation must be played against the need for an underlying sense of value and mission. The drive for results must take place by capturing the commitment of people rather than resorting to short-run exploitation. Decisions have to be made. Vacillating or languishing too long in an indecisive turmoil is a formula for competitive stagnation.

The issues have never been more demanding. How do we address the challenges of global competition? How do we find and keep the talent we need? How will technology reshape our industry? Given the expanding "gray area" of business, how will we even know whether our decisions are successes or mistakes? They may seem like acceptable decisions, but only time will tell if they are good enough. The stakes have never been higher. And the novelty and uncertainty of each issue twists the odds of reading everything "just right" lower and lower.

Against this maze of tensions, someone must see that the right things get done. That someone is the leader. On the leader's shoulders sits the responsibility of sifting through complexities, charting a course, and moving the organization's people in a new direction. There are few greater challenges and few greater struggles. Given all of this, it's not surprising that leadership is a key focus in contemporary organizations.

The Organization's Many Leaders

Mike works for a mid-sized service business. He is neither the CEO nor the president. In fact, he holds no lofty position of formal authority. His title, Project Manager, conveys little about the real nature and range of his impact.

Like so many throughout the organizational world, Mike is a great follower. While he politely accepts the periodic praise and recognition of his superiors, being in the limelight is not a priority. He cares about his work and performs his assignments with energy and commitment. Yet, he's not flashy. There is no hidden agenda. He's a cog in a complex business doing the best he can.

But there is more. At 34 years old, Mike has an amazing capacity to connect with people. Perhaps, it's because of his open and friendly style, his clear-cut competence, or his personal work ethic that tries to ensure that every job is done just right. Whatever the reason, people like him. And they turn to him with questions and problems. Mike listens, asks questions, and offers suggestions. He supports people and tells them when they've done a good job. He shows empathy and encourages them. While Mike doesn't do others' "dirty work" for them, he doesn't shy away from issues and controversies.

Through his interactions with others, Mike builds a stronger organizational community, and he helps people to work more effectively and feel better about what they do. It is not an overstatement to say that he inspires those around him. By any reasonable definition, Mike is a leader. His leadership has nothing to do with his title or his organizational position, which is undesignated and unclear as one peruses the organizational chart. His leadership comes through contact. It is earned in a planning session by the strength and logic of his arguments. It is earned by the way he supports a colleague because her presentation "just makes sense." It is earned in the lunchroom as he casually but sincerely asks a project manager from a different unit how his wife's radiation treatment is going.

Typically, powerful and positive leader role models are unsung heroes. They are the good soldiers who do not make the press. Most important, leaders are not simply those who sit at the top of the organization; they exist at all levels. Anyone who works with and through others to get desired action is using leadership. Sometimes, as we saw with Mike, the most influential leaders are not those with the most impressive titles or the broadest span of control. In fact, one of the critical needs of contemporary businesses is to build deep cadres of leaders throughout the organization.

The organization is the sole vehicle by which a corporation fulfills its mission and achieves its vision. The brightest and most skilled surgeons in the world cannot perform their marvels independent of the health care organization in which they work. Nor can the president of the United States, the university professor, or the corporate CEO succeed without an effective functioning organization. It's the organization that allows them to be successful. Therefore, one of any leader's tasks is to make an effective organization.

Consequently, there is a need for what might best be called *the leader-follower chain* within every organization. Every leader has a group of followers, each of those followers serve as leaders to another group of followers, and so on until practically everyone in the organization serves in some capacity as both leader and follower.

There seems to be some stigma attached to the word *follower*. Nevertheless, good leaders learn by first becoming good followers. That is, they master the skills of working cooperatively and collaboratively with their peers. They develop the habit of respect and learn how to recognize and express appreciation for the contributions of others. Followers learn how to set aside their personal needs and agendas for the greater good or goal. They are hardly passive donkey-like individuals, but are actively engaged in assisting the leader implement corporate strategy. They know their power is based in their knowledge, skills, creativity, and motivation. They are not dependent creatures. They realize that the leader ultimately depends upon them if success is to be achieved.

There is no such thing as one leader in an organization. Leaders permeate the organization whether they have the title of CEO, vice-president, director, supervisor, team leader, or coordinator. Their task is also to lead, to mobilize their respective part of the organization's talent force to fulfill the corporate mission and implement its strategies.

Attila or Matilda the Hun leadership is toxic leadership. It has no place in the modern corporation. The knowledge and information-based economy requires a different kind of leadership. No one person can possess all the knowledge, skills, and information needed to manage an organization. However, like the conductor of a multi-talented orchestra, the leader must know how to bring out the best in people and recognize their unique contributions. The leader insures that they all play in harmony and inspires confidence and pride in doing it well. Leaders must have passion for their work; without passion, nothing great will ever be achieved. Above all, leaders must express appreciation for work well done by their followers.

As one of our leaders said: "It's people, people, people." Again, we can't emphasize this enough. Effective leaders know how to work well with others. They know how to work cooperatively, collaboratively, and supportively with others. And they show appreciation and give recognition. This is the kind of leadership required from everyone in the organizational leader-follower chain.

The Life of the Leader

There is more than this in the life of the leader. There is a deeper and more profound theme that confronts today's leaders. And unless this theme is consciously incorporated into a manager's leadership identity, misery lies ahead.

Leadership, by its very nature, is intertwined with adversity. Recall the classic work of Henry Mintzberg. Mintzberg categorized the work of leading into 10 roles. One of these leader roles is "disturbance handler." Here, the leader deals with crises, often arising from unforeseen events. Mintzberg noted when a crisis is present, the disturbance handler role is given precedence over all others.[2]

The mantle of leadership is tough and demanding. It's about struggle and adversity. Importantly, it's about stepping up and stepping through the landmines scattered in the field. It's recognizing that missteps will occur and that there will be damage. And it's recognizing that there must be the capacity and the resiliency to move ahead. This journey can be all–consuming, draining the leader to the point of surrender.

Let's be clear. When such adversities strike, some leaders walk away. They become resentful, bitter shells of who they were and who they want to be. Yet there is another option. The struggles of adversity can be a challenge, pumping energy into the leader and bringing personal significance and contentment.

These are two dramatically different outcomes. One displays a picture of desperation, the other pounds with hope and satisfaction. One is spiraling toward personal failure; the other is the life–source of personal success.

We are convinced that one of the keys differentiating these outcomes is how mistakes, adversities, and crises are recognized and addressed. In fact, leadership grows from adversity.

Adversities shape and develop leaders. One of the leaders we interviewed, in his straightforward style, said it best: "The village idiot can lead when everything's going along great. It's when things aren't so great that we find out what kind of leaders we are. That's when we really show our leadership."

———————— *The Wisdom of Experience* ————————

The very nature of leadership is demanding and involves struggles and managing those struggles. It is in this cauldron of adversity that the mettle of leadership is forged. A lot of it has to do with people, which is always a tricky business. In the end, all leadership revolves around the ability to mobilize people to achieve a common goal. There is no easy way of doing this—it always takes hard work.

No organization can be successful without multiple leaders functioning throughout the organization. We are not addressing just the CEO, but every leader within the organization. At least part of what distinguishes successful leaders from others is how these leaders address their mistakes, adversities, and crises—how they bounce back or rebound from setbacks. How this rebound is accomplished is laid out in the chapters that follow.

3

The Experience of Success

"Have a goal, work hard, have fun, and always give more than you get. If you do all of those things, you're going to be successful."

Many of the leaders we interviewed were bothered by our decision to label them as a "success." By most external indicators or obvious benchmarks, these were successful people. Yet, the term itself created an intriguing struggle as leaders applied it to their own experiences.

It was against this backdrop that we began our interviews by asking participants what *success* meant to them. Some were caught off-guard by this unexpected and rather philosophic opening. Most were highly reflective and even profound. Some, like the leader quoted in the following example, offered penetrating insights.

"Interesting question. I don't feel that successful." Sitting across from this accomplished leader, it was clear that these were not simply idle words or some self-deprecating move designed to suggest a commendable level of humility. No, these words were carefully chosen and deeply felt expressions of honest emotion.

"The term causes me to think I've arrived. I don't think I've arrived. I've got a lot more work to do." There was a spunky defensiveness in these phrases. But then, with a decidedly serious tone, he continued, "To some people, success means money and achievement from a career standpoint. That's not how I view it—not how I gauge success. I think of it as making a difference. I feel privileged to be in a position to make a difference. I feel proud to have the ability to do some good—to be able to affect changes that are needed.

"Success is more internal than how other people view it. Success means contributing. Can I contribute something and in the end make a difference? Can I make a difference in my family, in my business, and in my community?

"I've always been involved in creating something. I like the part about doing things that can't get done—where the odds are very slim. And then the fulfillment comes from contributing, to getting the impossible or difficult accomplished, that makes a difference for people. Yep, making a difference, I think, sums it up for me."

Public or External Success

In a very basic way, success has both a public (external) and personal (internal) face. First, there is a social or external basis for success. Here, others ascribe or designate one as a success, presumably based on tangible public accomplishments.

For example, Lou Gerstner is viewed as a success because he was able to take a blue-chip company like IBM and turn it from a relatively static dinosaur to a lively, aggressive, fast-paced market winner. Jack Welch consistently led GE toward innovation with impressive growth and earnings. Financial guru Richard Driehaus experienced unparalleled performance of his portfolios. Such external measures of success, drawn from a track record of performance, are rather easy to discern.

Success is a function of goals and perceived attainment. Success comes from setting worthwhile goals (usually professional goals) and achieving them. The logic is simple. It is tough to feel successful if goals remain unfulfilled, if performance outcomes are lacking, and if the business has dramatically underachieved. Public success provides a common standard or barometer of achievement.

The interviewed leaders' words were clear: "Pretty much planning and accomplishing some of the things I planned for. That's the base of success." "Set some internal goals . . . accomplish them, reach a bit further than I did before. That's when I feel good."

Personal or Internal Success—The Sense of Personal Significance

The internal dimension of success is different. It is a personal sense. For most of us, it is drawn from a broader scale than simply looking at work-related achievements. Even within the work climate, the measuring stick may be much different since a leader knows what could have been, what actually was missed, and how far outcomes truly varied from plans and expectations. Conceivably, leaders could have considerable trappings of achievement, leading to a designation of external success, yet, in private, still question their self-worth and success. What is seen by others and felt by the leader can be two different realities.

Edwin Arlington Robinson's poem, "Richard Cory", dramatically portrays the difference between what others see and one might feel:

> Whenever Richard Cory went down town,
> We people on the pavement looked at him:
> He was a gentleman from sole to crown,
> Clean favored, and imperially slim.
>
> And he was always quietly arrayed,
> And he was always human when he talked;
> But still he fluttered pulses when he said,
> "Good morning," and he glittered when he walked.
>
> And he was rich—yes richer than a king—
> And admirably schooled in every grace:
> In fine, we thought that he was everything
> To make us wish that we were in his place.
>
> So on we worked, and waited for the light,
> And went without the meat, and cursed the bread;
> And Richard Cory, one calm summer night,
> Went home and put a bullet through his head.

Obviously something was missing. This something is particularly important for our purposes, and we have labeled it the "sense of personal significance." In short, this view maintains that success is less a function of what has been achieved than how one feels about what has been achieved. While public success may be an important measuring stick, the essence of success resides in the sense of personal significance.

As we have worked with organizational people at all levels and have studied the motivational literature, we are struck by the power of personal significance.[1] It is not unique to leaders. It occurs irrespective of position.

This sense of significance may be the most powerful motivator affecting any of us. Significance occurs when people feel that they make a difference—that their contribution, regardless of how slight it may be, adds value to what is being done. The leaders in our study viewed success as a function of personal significance. Listen to their language:

"I want our business to make a contribution . . . Our contribution has to be with our customer . . . And the only way to contribute to the customer's life is to make a contribution to our employees' lives and add value to the most important asset we have: our people. And they add value to the customer. So success, in my opinion, is not being the biggest or making the most money, but making the most contribution."

Another leader offered, "To me success is more about achieving goals and thereby achieving satisfaction . . . It occurs when you feel that satisfaction of someone (an employee) doing so well." Or, as another responded, "Success, professionally, indicates that you can see very vividly where you have been instrumental in improving the lives and careers of those people around you. Success, personally, is not measured in dollars and cents. It's measured in having successful projects, programs, and seeing the fruits of a lot of work and effort do something meaningful in the marketplace, and of course, in your place of business."

Consider the succinct logic as another leader pondered the nature of success, "I contributed something, and in the end I made a difference. To me that is success . . . I made a difference—in my family . . . in my business . . . in my community."

Finally, look at the clear perspective offered by this leader, "At the end of the run, whatever position you had, can you really look back and say to yourself, 'Am I proud of what I've accomplished?' If you can answer that positively, then it doesn't matter to me what anyone else thinks. I mean you want your family to be proud of you, you want your community to be proud of you, but it really doesn't begin to count until you've met your own criteria."

As you can see, the leaders' views of success were profoundly personal, and revolved around the sense of personal significance. In short, success is experienced through actions and contributions that provide personal significance. Let us repeat our first point here. We will drive this point home because it speaks volumes about success, and it speaks volumes about adversity: *Success is less a function of what has been achieved and more a function of how you assess and feel about what has been achieved.*

The Wisdom of Experience

Success means many things to many people, but for our leaders it came down to one simple internal evaluation of how well they met their personal criteria for success. It had little to do with the public's judgment of their work.

As a matter of fact, all of the leaders we interviewed had already been acknowledged in myriad ways as being successful; it was one of the criteria for being included in this book. But what really mattered was how they judged themselves in their own eyes and by their own standards.

At issue was whether they made a difference in the life of their customers, employees, family, or friends. And they were hard evaluators. No one gave themselves a perfect "10." Yet this was never a source of dissatisfaction, but seemed to serve as a stimulus for improvement. Nevertheless, the key to long-term success depends on how well the leader responds to adversity.

4

The Paradox of Success

"It's a heck of a victory because it was a heck of a fight."

A bove the doors entering the Congressional Reading Room of the Library of Congress are nine paintings. Known as the Hall of Heroes, these paintings depict episodes in the lives of mythological figures. Hercules, Odysseus, Achilles, Paris, Jason, Theseus, Bellerophon, Orpheus, and Prometheus are all represented in the Hall. But what is their purpose?

These episodes exist as allegories. As such, each episode speaks to the human condition. Each has a central theme that revolves around risk, fear, and human faults and frailties. Each provides a lesson about confronting danger and overcoming fear. Courage and conviction in the face of adversity distinguishes each hero. More deeply, these stories demonstrate that the trials and tribulations that stand between all heroes and their destinies are the very tests that shape character and enable dreams to be fulfilled.

Taken as a whole, it is a lesson about the courage needed to confront evil and wrongdoing, the dangers involved in doing so, and the fears to be overcome as the hero challenges an opponent. They serve as reminders and sources of inspiration to the members of Congress as they pass through these doors of what will be demanded of them as leaders of our nation. Do they have the determination, the steadfastness, the courage and the conviction to overcome the obstacles and meet the challenges that lie before them? It is a test of their mettle, their character.

The Connection Between Success and Adversity

We experience the same dynamics. We are all engaged in a quest to fulfill our dreams, to capture a vision of what we want for ourselves professionally and personally. Yet, there is no guarantee in life that what we pursue will be achieved. Success is not a given.

There is a deep dimension, a revealing connection between success and adversity. It is truly paradoxical. The very nature of success implies failure, and any claim to success without a risk of failure is nothing less than self-deception and personal fraud.

There is no such thing as success if there is nothing to overcome. In fact, the essence of success, that sense of personal significance, is strangely defined through the experience of adversity. We refer to it as the **Paradox of Success:** *The meaning and value of success are heightened as adversity experiences increase and intensify.*

One of the leaders we interviewed was a talented entrepreneur who had built a large and respected national service business. He spoke of a pattern of success: "When we started the business . . . I said to anybody that would listen that we were going to be a million–dollar company. That was the wildest thing you could have imagined. The people around me couldn't believe it. They'd laugh . . . achieving that goal was probably the best thing that's ever happened to me. Then I figured, well, my life is over! I needed things to do, and I'd done it. All our people had done it. We had a big party. We celebrated, and it was fun. But now where do you go?

"'Finally,' I said to myself, 'I'll never make a goal that easy again in my whole life.' The next goal was $10 million. Now you should have heard people laugh. You should have seen their reactions . . . We finally made it, and then we came to the realization that life is really achieving goals. So once we made that $10 million goal, I said, 'I'll never do that again because it's too easy.' The next goal was $100 million. . . After that, the goal was $300 million . . . Now we're working on $1 billion."

At each step along the way, he shared the struggles. He spoke of nearly going broke. He spoke of the long, trying process of courting investors. He spoke of critical turns in market structure that were nearly disastrous. He noted that there were times when both he and the business were fighting for their lives. As we talked, he presented a profound perspective: "I think a lot of people who are successful are kind of at the fringe of society . . . They aren't members of the masses who are conformists. They do things their own way. They do things differently."

It was clear that he understood and accepted adversity and struggle as part of the process of succeeding. More importantly, he expressed a growing maturity that enabled him to step forward with unbelievable (yes, even laughable) goals for the future. And he recognized that his achievements, his very success, had meaning and significance precisely because of the adversities that he had addressed.

Another example, from a totally different arena, is Lance Armstrong's 1999 Tour de France victory, which many consider one of the greatest sports achievements in history. Others have won the Tour, some under much more grueling conditions. But Armstrong's performance epitomizes success because of the crisis he confronted.

In 1996, he was diagnosed with testicular cancer that had spread to his abdomen, lungs, and brain. Even with aggressive treatment, doctors placed his odds of survival at no better than 50–50. For the next year, he fought back, battled the cancer, and endured the draining effects of rehabilitation. Two years later, after 22 days and over 2,000 miles of racing against the top cyclists in the world, he rode through the streets of Paris victoriously. All the trauma, pain, unlikely odds, and unparalleled dedication gave his triumph added meaning. The crisis, and his response to it, had raised his success to a higher level.

Personal Significance and Adversity

Leaders feel alive; they feel energized; and they gain their greatest sense of personal significance when they have to battle through tough times and events. This is where they make a difference. This is where their unique talents are put to the test. This is where they step up and respond.

In many ways, this is where they distinguish themselves from the masses. As one senior executive noted, "Leadership is earned when things are falling apart." This leader went on to describe two major business crises, each affecting the very nature and survival of the business. He explained that these two events were his greatest trials and, consequently, his greatest successes. It was in dealing with and moving through these times that he earned his greatest sense of personal significance and his greatest sense of success.

Believing the Paradox

One of the most creative and charismatic leaders we interviewed boasted an impressive 20-year history of business success. Rapid expansion and double-digit growth had marked most years. Against this positive backdrop, the last two years had stood in stark contrast. They were years of high–profile setbacks. Two major projects had gone bad, each gaining considerable public exposure. A personal health crisis had required extensive hospitalization. A restructuring of the leadership team had taken place.

We were not quite sure what to expect as we began our interview to explore dimensions of success. We were greeted with a remarkable, even surprising, display of commitment and resilience. Describing the advances and accomplishments of the past six months, this leader made it clear that for him, recent successes held special meaning and special significance: "I think the best things happen when some crisis or disaster challenges us."

There was a lot to that statement. For this leader, it rang true. Success was sweeter because of what had occurred and what had been overcome. The paradox had legitimacy precisely because it had been experienced.

The Wisdom of Experience

The very definition of success implies achievement, obstacles to be overcome, and a real possibility of failure. The greater the success, the greater are the obstacles to that success, and the greater the possibility of failure. There is no such thing as success if there's nothing to overcome.

In the face of adversity, courage and steadfastness are required of us. It is a time of great temptation to run, hide, and give-up. But this is a very internal journey, and only those who have traveled it know how well they have measured up. These are the times in life when our character and our leadership potential are either strengthened or weakened. Adversity is either a time of growth, or a time of personal setback.

THE ANATOMY OF ADVERSITY

5

The Nature of Adversity

"There is just one small step between success and failure."

Gary was a competent and talented engineer. He boasted a number of achievements. He had risen quickly through his mid-sized organization. In his early forties, with a strong technical background, it certainly appeared he was being groomed to assume the presidency of the business within a few years. He had taken on increasing management responsibilities. While keeping his hands on a few pet projects, most of his time over the past six months was devoted to his growing leadership role. He entered our "Emerging Leaders" program with a promising profile—a young, bright, fast tracker about to take a key step up in his leadership journey.

Gary had difficulty getting away from work for our meeting. His prevailing desire was to get back to his office as soon as he could. That probably explained why small talk was limited, and he jumped right into his concerns: "I sure do waste a lot of time dealing with other people's problems. They always want my view or my read on something. Sometimes it just seems like the issues are so clear. All they want is somebody to hold their hand. It sure makes it tough to get my work done."

These words, expressed with a different tone or inflection, may have offered little insight. But this was not the case. His words carried a caustic and bitter tone. And there was more. There was anger.

Over the next hour, we discussed Gary's career and his progress. He delighted in the technical challenges of his work. He enjoyed the demands and sense of accomplishment that came as he completed important projects. But he chafed at the demands of leadership, which by its very nature involves dealing with people. He saw many of the interpersonal contacts as unnecessary inconveniences and distractions. And that attitude was increasingly apparent to his peers and his direct reports.

Gary was confronting a major struggle in his life as a leader. He was grappling with a critical decision. Gary faced a career crisis unlike any he had previously known. He was torn between the technical work he loved and the emerging leadership role his superiors wanted him to play.

At one level, as a bright man, Gary was aware of what was happening. Yet, in a very real way, he was completely unaware of what was going on. He felt the stress. He knew work was less fun. But he never fully acknowledged, thought through, and addressed the crisis before him. He responded in the only way he knew how—he hunkered down and worked harder and longer. Of course, these actions served as evidence to his bosses that Gary had what it took to handle the demands of leadership. So, they expanded his leadership role.

Through this process, Gary was changing. He was moving from an upbeat, steady, positive person to something else. He spent more time alone in his office. He became irritated at small project delays that earlier would have been addressed and taken in stride. Rather than playing his typical mentoring and teaching roles, he now lashed out at coworkers for their mistakes. His home life was affected as the frustrations of the day spilled over on his wife and kids, furthering his frustration, guilt, and anger. As I suggested to Gary that he faced a critical career test, he nodded.

The Levels of Adversity

Just as success has both personal and public components, adversity is always a struggle at two levels: personal (internal) and public (external). Effective resolution of any crisis or adverse event requires that both levels be managed simultaneously. For example, leaders are public figures. Despite their personal struggles, the business must move ahead. The real world has its own demands which cannot be ignored. However, the internal or personal level is the center from which all adversity is conquered. This is where issues are emotionally felt and mentally sifted and sorted.

The heart of adversity is always a personal battle. While adversity may have a public face, it must be confronted and addressed at the personal level. For successful leaders, adversity is not so much a function of what has happened, but how adversity's events affect and move them at a personal level.

Categories of Adversity

Experience teaches us that no one's life and leadership journey is free from disappointments, frustrations, obstacles, and crises. They come in a variety of forms: death, illness, financial loss, divorce, angry employees, interpersonal conflicts, ethical challenges, and jealousies. All are events that can block the leader's path to success. No one is spared. Like death and taxes, adversity is a constant.

Not only is adversity a given, but in today's turbulent and chaotic business environment, adversities seem to appear with more frequency and intensity than ever. As one executive noted, "They just seem to crop up more. And the lows seem lower."

Sifting through our interviews, we sought logical and meaningful ways to categorize leaders' adversities—their misfortunes, trials, and tribulations. We drew interpretations from our analysis and from careful consideration of the previous work in the adversity field. Typically, adversities fall into one of three categories—business, career, or personal.[1] Each category may have many bases.

Categories of Adversities

Business Adversities	Career Adversities	Personal Adversities
Mistakes and Missteps	Missed Promotions and Key Assignments	Leader and Family Health Issues
Volatility of Business Environment	Change in Career	Family Relationship Issues
Interpersonal or People Issues	Getting Fired	

Business Adversities

Business adversities were mentioned frequently by the leaders in our study. Business adversities ranged from minor irritations to intense concerns. In general, these adversities fell into one of three categories: mistakes and missteps, volatility of the business environment, and interpersonal or people-oriented issues.

1. Mistakes and Missteps. Business adversities may arise from the mistakes and missteps that inevitably come as one performs the duties of leadership. Leaders will make mistakes. Those who do not err are playing it so safely that they have already abdicated their roles as leaders.

Leaders are expected to address opportunities, read situations, and act. But they will misstep; they will make mistakes; and they will face the troubling consequences of these decisions and actions. As we all know, the world of leadership is one of stepping up and making tough calls with imperfect and incomplete information. Failure to do so results in stagnation. Further, leaders deal with the "gray area" where right and wrong decisions are often shaded and may not be fully revealed until some years down the line.

It was stated simply by the CEO of a fast-growth firm who talked about the complexity of leading today and the reality of making mistakes: "None of us are smart enough to make every decision correctly." He went on to say that he hoped to make more good than bad decisions, to be able to honestly admit the bad ones, move quickly to fix them, learn what had happened, and not make the same mistake twice. While expressed in his own words, he was describing the fundamental reality of leader mistakes.

Another leader commented, "When you get tough decisions, you've got to make them before you have all the facts. Sometimes we only have half the facts, and sometimes we've only got 10 percent of the facts. I think the worst thing a leader could do is wait until they have all the facts—which usually never comes." In short, leaders face business adversities because of the mistakes they make while performing their leader roles. Successful leaders understand that doing the right thing is no guarantee against misfortune.

2. Volatility of the Business Environment. At times, leaders face business adversity simply because of the tenuous and uncertain nature of working in today's dynamic and volatile business environment. Even the best calculations can go awry.

One of our leaders drove this point home with a wonderful story from his childhood. With a twinkle in his eye, he recalled his experience as a boy. "The family played cards, and we always played for money—not much, but enough to keep the game interesting. Well, I get this hand, and I'm beside myself. I can't lose. I mean, even as a kid I could calculate the odds. There's only one card that can beat me. Twenty cards have been dealt. There's only one chance out of the remaining 32 that I don't win. And the pot is pretty big. I run into my room and get all my paper route money and toss it in. And guess what? I'm dealt that one card. Unreal. I'm devastated. I'm crying. Wow, what a lesson! Was that a bad decision? Of course not. It was the right decision. I'd play those same odds the same way every time. Sometimes the right decision just gives you crummy outcomes."

As he retold the story, he noted that it was a lesson he had never forgotten. It taught him two things. First, don't take the risk if you can't live with the consequences. Second, and most important, sometimes you make the best call you can and adversity still comes. Given the nature of today's business environment, laden with uncertainty and volatility, good decisions can still yield undesirable results.

3. Interpersonal or People-Oriented Issues. A surprising number of business adversities revolved around people issues and interpersonal decisions. Gary's problems centered around his incapacity to deal with interpersonal issues. This isn't surprising when we consider that top derailers of leaders, according to research from the Center for Creative Leadership, are breakdowns in the interpersonal arena.[2]

Interestingly, when we asked leaders to describe their most personally rewarding and disappointing business experiences, both had to do with people issues. Generally, we heard of the disappointment of key people not performing as had been expected and interpersonal conflicts that demanded the leader's time and attention. At times, we heard of unacceptable breaches of company standards or ethical stances and breakdowns in trust. These may be common adversities but they are difficult.

Try as we might, these issues are personal and emotional because they involve real people. A number of leaders spoke of having to replace a key member of the management team. Although these decisions were made for logical business reasons, the impact was dramatic and emotional precisely because it was a people issue. These were the issues that seemed to take the greatest toll on our participants.

Career Adversities

Career adversities involve a break in the leader's expected pattern of career progress. It may be relatively minor, such as not being selected for a particular assignment or project. It may be more serious and involve missing a key promotion. In some cases, it may involve a change in careers. Finally, it may even involve getting fired.

At some point, most leaders, even highly successful leaders, struggle with such career adversities. Career adversities may be so subtle that their full impact is clouded by the day-to-day actions of leadership.

1. Missed Promotions and Key Assignments. Reflecting over their careers, a number of leaders in our study recounted situations where promotions and desired, high profile assignments were anticipated but did not occur. Here, adversity was experienced because the leaders' career expectations were blocked or thrown off course.

Leaders experienced an array of emotions when promotion or assignment opportunities were thwarted. Some were angry, some were deeply disappointed, and some were simply confused. Yet, all the leaders felt the experience of adversity because a personal indicator of career progress and success had not fallen in place.

In hindsight, many leaders realized that being "skipped" for a promotion or seeing an offer for a key project assignment extended to another employee might have been reasonable from a broad organizational point of view. As one leader noted, "I wanted it [new assignment and promotion]. I'd worked hard and had some good success. When it didn't come, I was pretty upset...Actually, looking back, I wasn't ready, and my boss knew it." While this leader noted that he probably knew, even at the time, that his boss had made the right decision, "being passed over was crushing."

2. Change in Career. Nearly half of the leaders we studied experienced a significant shift or change in their careers. In some cases, this decision merely involved changing companies. For some, there was a shift to an entirely new industry with a new set of professional activities.

The timing of the career change decision was quite varied. Often, the decision to pursue a different career direction came early, while the leaders were relatively young. But this certainly was not the rule. A number of leaders made the career change decision in their late thirties or forties.

Generally, the decision to change career was prompted by one of two factors: dissatisfaction or opportunity. In conditions of dissatisfaction, the leaders were unhappy with the way career events and prospects were unfolding. In conditions of opportunity, the leaders recognized the presence of a more promising career alternative. Logically, dissatisfaction and opportunity were linked. As leaders experienced dissatisfaction with their career direction, they either searched for or became more sensitive to other opportunities.

Regardless of its underlying cause, career change involves a disruption. New experience, training, and learning must be endured. In many cases, a career change requires relocation, with all the family implications such a move involves. Even when the career change is positive, exciting, and beneficial, the move from an established pattern to something different brings uncertainty, risk, and stress.

3. Getting Fired. Several of the participants in our study had been fired at some point in their careers. Needless to say, termination is hardly a pleasant life event. One leader captured the overall impact of getting fired as he commented, "It's a hell of a way to grow but grow you do." Logically, termination is an event that has to be resolved if one is to succeed in the next position.

Getting fired is an extreme form of adversity for the obvious personal reasons. Questions of competence and an uncertain future logically arise. Yet, termination has an even more dramatic impact because it is a public display.

Personal Adversities

The leaders in our study, while a personally hardy group, experienced their typical share of personal adversities. While obvious, this point is often missed. Successful leaders experience the same kinds of personal trials and demands as everyone else in the organization.

1. Leader and Family Health Issues. The most common personal adversities were health concerns affecting the leader or a very close member of the leader's family. These events are troubling for two reasons. First, a health concern, by its very nature, carries a certain amount of trauma and anxiety. Second, however, is that a leader must ensure that the organization continues to perform as these health issues unfold.

Even relatively minor personal health concerns can take time, attention, and energy from the normal course of work activities. As the seriousness of the health issue rises, the tension between work and that issue intensifies. Not surprisingly, a number of leaders noted that they felt more comfortable handling their personal health concerns than they were when the health of others was involved. This may be due to a greater sense of perceived control over personal versus others' issues.

2. Family Relationship Issues. Family relationship issues usually had to do with marital strains and problems with children. The leaders' comments on family adversities offered an interesting but not unexpected connection. Overwhelmingly, when asked how important family was to their personal sense of success, our leaders placed family at the top, either above or on par with their careers. Yet, when asked where the most troubling sacrifices had come as they achieved career success, they pointed to family.

Crises–A Question of Survival

Admittedly, there is a fine perceptual line between adversity and crisis. Indeed one leader's adversity may be another's crisis. For our purposes, an adversity becomes a crisis when there is a question of survival.

For example, a business crisis exists when there is a direct and real threat to the long-run viability of the business or some phase of the business. Logically, a series of interlocking mistakes can lead to a crisis. As one leader noted, "We committed big bucks to this venture. We leveraged our core business to support the promise of this venture. . . Things went sour . . . and our core business was vulnerable." Or as another noted with straightforward candor, "Bankruptcy was very real . . . It was sheer survival. [I thought] I can't let this go down. Somehow, I've got to figure this out."

In a similar vein, career adversities become crises when there is a threat that career momentum and direction will have to shift. Again, it becomes an issue of survival. This was the case with Gary, in our opening scenario.

In fact, Gary's promotion to a leadership position is not an unusual example. He discovered or at least experienced that leadership required paying attention to and managing the human factors of his followers. He would never succeed unless he developed the skills to do this. And yet he found his whole being pulled away from that very task. He faced a career crisis, since the entire direction and nature of his career was being challenged.

Similar to what we have said for the business and career categories, a personal crisis exits when there is a threat to personal survival or the survival of key relationships. Serious illnesses, marital discord, and potential divorce were the prominent examples. We encountered a number of personal crises throughout our study. As expected, the impact was often profound. Such crises often prompted a reexamination of priorities.

The Ties between Adversities

Of course, no leader's life is so structured and segmented that they have the luxury of addressing one challenge at a time. Like all of us, the categories affect one another. The unique role of leadership demands that we keep going even as adversity builds.

Even as personal crisis looms, the business has to keep going. It is interesting that Disney CEO Michael Eisner reports giving business instructions and detailing his succession plan as he was being wheeled into surgery following his heart attack.[3]

This spillover is important because of the additive nature of adversity. Adversities can pile up and push one to the level of crisis. While no single adversity may reach the crisis threshold, when considered collectively, a crisis looms in the leader's eyes.

—————— *The Wisdom of Experience* ——————

Adversity is just a fact of life. Yes, it's an external event that demands resolution. But there are internal ramifications, collateral damage to the psyche so to speak. One's sense of significance—the ability to make a difference—is also under assault. And sooner or later, adversity comes to everyone in one form or another: business, career, or personal. Those who are sensitive to this as an inevitable reality of either their business or personal existence seem more able to adjust to it when it does occur.

It is not so much the event, but how that event is experienced and mentally dealt with that determines the degree of adversity. When it is viewed as a threat to survival, we are dealing with something more. That is called a crisis. But no matter what the adversity, the responsibility of leadership requires that the leader also attend to the daily demands of the business and family.

In the end, adversity is a matter of the psyche or soul. That is where the battle is either won or lost. This is where the real test of character occurs. And it is the nature of this battle that we will explore in our later chapters.

6

The Tests of Adversity

"I can't let this go down. Somehow, I've got to figure this out."

Listen to the emotion expressed by a company president as he recounted the personal struggle of losing a major customer. "We lost a big account. That was really frightening. I can still remember . . . my last visit there, trying to hang on to it. They brought the business in-house. It wasn't that they were unhappy with us. I was forced to cut my people, which didn't make me too happy. And it turned out that we replaced them many-fold. But at the time, things like that are devastating. To lose a company [like that] is frightening, very frightening. They have been replaced, but at the time, I didn't know if they could be [replaced] or not. And just the thought of losing a nice big account, you know, what are people going to think. . . I still remember that day."

You can find similar examples by perusing the pages of the *Wall Street Journal* or *Business Week*. Numerous stories exemplify the adversities that today's business leaders must face. Nike reports a dramatic 30 percent decline in its third quarter earnings. Goldman Sachs experiences consecutive quarters of sliding profits. Silicon Valley giants Intel and Cisco Systems dramatically shave their workforces in the face of softening markets.

Although we are unaware of all the details, we recognize that these business adversities demand actions from the companies' leaders. Of course, we only see part of the struggle. While these business events unfold, a myriad of personal and career adversities also spin on. While leader decisions are played out in the public arena, we recognize, intuitively, that considerable struggle certainly preceded those decisions. The decision to trim the payroll may be a fundamental business action, but it's clear that a lot of churning went into the decision.

However, there is an even deeper piece to the adversity puzzle, one that we rarely see: the components of adversity and crisis that touch leaders at their deepest and most personal level. Make no mistake, as we've said earlier, adversity is always addressed and wrestled with at the personal level. It's just a piece that generally isn't brought into the open. However, the leaders we interviewed did talk about these personal experiences, and their revelations are powerful.

Significance and Control

Adversities are troubling events because they rattle and shake two foundations that leaders hold near and dear: personal significance and sense of control. Adversities stand as tests of the leaders' belief and pride that they do make a positive difference. Adversity draws into question the perplexing inquiry, "If I can't control it, what good am I?"

For example, one CEO in our study, a highly accomplished and successful middle-aged leader, described his reaction to a business crisis: "Maybe I'm not capable. Maybe I'm not qualified. Maybe I'm not involved enough. Maybe I'm not doing enough. Maybe I'm not asking the right questions. Maybe I'm one of those guys who can't get it done."

Despite a string of business successes, adversity still evoked this deep confrontation. Each of his "maybe I . . ." statements questioned his significance. Such questions are not surprising, and they certainly are not unusual. Adversity causes us to question who we are. It causes us to question if we're any good. It raises self-doubt. Regardless of the bold image that may be projected, there is an internal tinge of uncertainty. During adversity, one's sense of significance is threatened.

Adversity also affects control. Leaders need to be in control; it is comforting and logical to believe that control exists. And, to a large extent, control is expected. Many leaders play games of self-deception to convince themselves that they have the capacity to handle anything. To question control counters the image of power that defines their role as leader. During adversity, one's sense of control is threatened.

Control is an even more prevalent theme during crisis. In fact, each crisis contains a critical underlying theme that drives to the heart of control. The leader has never been there before; the territory is new and the landscape unfamiliar. Their sense of control is threatened because the dynamics of the situation have never been met on a personal level. Largely, forces beyond the leader are calling the shots.

While they have seen similar crises around them, the experience becomes unique when they are the recipient rather than the observer. "I've seen other people get passed over for promotion and get fired. Hey, I've been the one who made some of those decisions, but it's different when it happens to you."

One may counter that every adversity does not truly raise a question of significance and control. We contend that it is simply a matter of degree. Adversity, by its defining nature, does affect significance and control. Crisis, by its challenge to survival, presents a heightened sense of vulnerability. But, the pattern is the same. Significance and control are on the line.

The Emotions of Adversity

The tests of adversity threaten a leader's sense of significance and control and raise in the leader the emotion most strongly fought and denied—fear. Generally, leaders will not openly admit fear. It is not the appropriate public persona. Nevertheless, it is there. In analyzing the initial response that leaders made when asked to describe their pressing adversities and crises, we were amazed how often a statement of fear crept into their conversation. Often, they openly admitted to being frightened, as expressed by the president in the opening story. Sometimes, the admission was accompanied with a laugh and an attempt to minimize the emotional side of the experience. "I guess I may have been a little scared. Yea, I guess there was some fear there."

A few years ago, I met with the newly appointed president of a regional financial institution. His rise to the top had taken place after years of displaying a consistent track record of performance. This was a man who projected an aura of confidence and competence, qualities important for his position. As we sat in his office, our conversation turned to the special challenges he confronted in his new role.

This was a man of vision with an acute sense of his industry and what his organization needed to do to carve a winning piece of the market. Soon, our conversation turned to problems, adversities, and even a potential crisis that seemed to be looming on the horizon. "In this seat there's no one left to check off what's done. The strategies I accept will become actions. I'm ready for this, but I gotta tell you, that's pretty scary!"

It is tough for leaders to accept that adversities may prompt fear. The organizational world and certainly patterns of business success are not built around models of fear. Quite the contrary, we have culturally promoted an image that moves in exactly the opposite direction.

Tough, hard driving, and relentless, modern models of managerial success move with fearless abandon through a prickly maze of organizational issues. This model suggests that even if leaders are battered, they fearlessly move ahead. Of course, this model and image is incomplete and emotionally naïve. It is based on contorted logic purporting that denying fear will make it go away. Such logic is psychologically bankrupt. The fear is still there.

Consider another topic that is churning through every organization today: change. Over the past five years, we have worked with a number of organizations in the midst of difficult and groundbreaking change. In most cases, we have not been involved in the planning phases of change. Rather, we have been called in to help the organization and its people cope with the new organizational world that is arising because of change.

We begin by asking people what the change they face means to them. We push them to address why they are bothered by these changes. We attempt to bring people and managers to a point of personal awareness and acceptance. This point is often one of confrontation. These people really do dislike what is happening, and they really are resisting change, but they are concerned that they will be looked upon negatively if they actually admit it.

We address the audience from a personal and emotional level. "There's nothing wrong with the resistance you are feeling. It is reasonable. It's even expected given what you are going through." We present a well-recognized behavioral principle of change management. Resistance is a natural response given the uncertainty, disruption, confusion, and the effort and energy that change requires. Most participants find this comforting because it confirms and legitimizes what they are experiencing. We then lead them to define and unpack why resistance exits.

Scholars from the Harvard Business School have nearly a 30-year history in addressing this issue.[1] Drawing from their work, we pinpoint a broad, but pervasive factor behind most resistance—fear. Leaders fear they will not be able to cope, that established patterns and relationships will be altered, that they will be less effective or less valued in the new scheme than they were previously, and that they will somehow lose more than they gain.

The links between the change literature and our views of adversity are unmistakable. Adversity, like change, is a disruption and pushes us into an uncomfortable new arena—it causes us to question our values and ourselves.

In both conditions, we are vulnerable. In both cases, there is the strange emotion of fear. Few have the guts to stand up and face the fear. Defensive postures prevail. Some lash out. Others become more isolated.

It is not the presence of fear, but the reaction to fear that makes the difference. Consistently, we found that successful leaders coped with their fear in a progressive manner. They were not immobilized by fear. Fear did not hold them back or prevent them from taking tough and needed action. Rather, fear existed as an honest and natural emotion that was simply part of the adversity equation.

Responding to Fear

If fear is the underlying emotion, what do leaders need as they face that bleak emotion? Our answer is four-fold: logic, method, significance, and courage.

Logic is the basic need to get a handle on what is going on. It is the need to find some reasonable explanation of why this adversity or crisis is happening. In many ways, logic provides a semblance of control. Some of the uncertainty and ambiguity is removed if an understanding of the issues and events underlying the adversity can be gained. Logic provides a grounding and order that enables both action and acceptance.

Method is the way out. Method pieces the components of the adversity together and points to a possible direction for response.

Method includes a viable plan of action that can be employed to move through adversity and crisis. Since method provides leaders with an approach for taking action, they move from feeling like idle victims to being active problem solvers. For most, this begins to strip away fear as they gain control. As one leader noted, "The worse thing is not knowing what to do."

Significance is the sense of self-worth that comes when leaders realize that this adversity can be traversed. This comes from the past—the memory that other crises have been confronted. It is based on the notion that survival has prevailed in the face of crisis. Significance breeds hope. Significance leads to a confident sense of self-esteem that helps leaders encounter fear as a challenge rather than a debilitating presence.

Courage is the emotional resilience to move ahead with conviction and passion. Courage is more than an attitude or a sense of resolve. Courage is a response. Courage comes when the method is put into action. As such, courage becomes a transforming presence.

The Motivational Impact of Adversity

Adversity has its motivational impact on leaders precisely because of how it rattles the emotions. It threatens significance and robs control, but also forces one to confront and move through adversity. One must encounter fear to recognize that fear's paralyzing grip can invigorate the emotional presence to fight. This is why many leaders speak of being energized and becoming even more driven during adversity.

Don't miss the impact of this theme. Rather than being stymied by adversity, successful leaders often gain a surge of commitment to work through its perils. One leader framed it clearly: "When things are going along pretty well, I can lose interest. I mean I'm still involved and doing the things I have to, but I sort of ask 'Do they need me or could any number of guys do this.' But then this comes along. It's our biggest customer and we're at loggerheads and it's not going to go away, and the answer isn't obvious. You know, I'm all psyched. I guess I know that I'm on the seat here—on the line for our business."

This is an argument drawn from the pages of cognitive dissonance theory.[2] Basically, the threats of adversity are so aversive that they prompt leaders to act to eliminate their presence. The drive is to regain the sense of significance and control and to overcome the emptiness of fear. These are the tests of adversity. Threatened significance and control bring leaders to a state of energized motivation and, as we will discuss shortly, brings them to the edge of transformation. But, like any test, all do not get high marks.

Low Marks on the Test

There is a cold and harsh reality. While all face the tests of adversity and struggle along the path of leadership, all do not step up and respond to the challenge in a manner that yields "good" or constructive outcomes. Some people refuse to acknowledge and address the real issues of adversity. They battle on, blindly at times. Their approach is to beat back the adversity. Here, adversity does transform, but that transformation takes a discomforting turn.

While some learn and grow, others give up. While some are energized, others sink into depression. In the face of adversity, some leaders fold. Some display their true character, perhaps for the first time. At times, that penetrating glimpse of character is not pretty. For some, the tests of adversity are overwhelming, and the struggles throw them off course. For others, adversity brings forth bitterness, regressive ways of coping, and offers little real growth and development.

Faced with adversity and its accompanying tests, all are transformed. But, at least for some, that transformation brings unwanted outcomes.

Faced with adversity, why do some grow while others destruct? Much of this has to do with the way people look at and approach their challenges. It is, in many ways, an approach to adversity that recognizes the importance and necessity of the struggle.

One leader stated it well. Reflecting on his struggles, he noted, in a rather matter-of-fact style, "It's a serious disadvantage for life to be too good or too easy. If you have all victories, you're never prepared for defeat." Leadership is about struggle. Successful leaders experience their leadership mettle being forged in the crucible of crisis while others are blunted by the encounter. For them, adversity presents itself, and they go no further.

────────── *The Wisdom of Experience* ──────────

Adversity always occurs at a deeply personal level. In a way, adversity is an assault upon one's very sense of self, one's competency and adequacy. Our sense of significance is threatened and there is a feeling of loss of control. Fear strikes the heart although many pretend it doesn't.

People talk about resistance to change. In reality, this is just a more acceptable label for fear. The potential loss of power, relationships, comfort, and the challenge to do something different elicits feelings of fear as a natural biological reaction.

Some spend their time trying to chase fear away by pretending it's not within them. This approach boasts a bold image, yet the inner tension of fear remains. Importantly, the feelings of fear don't matter as much as how we confront fear. This is the first great test of adversity. That confrontation takes courage, for fear and courage are different realities. One is a feeling and the other an action.

The first step is to admit that one feels fear. By exploring the nature of those fears, the leader acquires a better understanding about the nature of the dragon. Paradoxically, this is the step to gaining control over the feelings of lost control and developing a plan of action.

7

The Adversity Cycle

"I view adversity as an interruption."

George Thomas is one of the world's finest athletes. He may lack the name recognition, but to those in his field, he is a giant of ultra-marathon bicycle racing. Ultra marathons are grueling long distance races, often nonstop, that test the mental and physical endurance of its participants. Some of the races, such as the fabled Race Across America, are staggering physical feats while others are just "short" jaunts—like the 500 miles from Kansas City to St. Louis that racers cover in around 30 hours, nonstop!

George not only competes in such unbelievable events, but he's often the winner. Frequently, he alone beats entire teams of other riders. George's victories are even more impressive when it's revealed that he is an epileptic.

When George was struck by a drunk driver, he was introduced to the confusing and draining world of epileptic seizures. His story of fight and resiliency in the face of adversity is remarkable. It's a story he recounts with candor and a certain disarming humor.

George took up bicycling as a form of therapy following the accident. When he talks about the pain of ultra marathon racing, he has perspective. When he talks about quitting and giving in to the pain, it's clear that he probably won't. As you listen to George talk, there is no doubt that the crises he has faced have changed and transformed him.

When George describes the 30th hour of a nonstop race, his body throbbing as the pain approaches the breaking point, we know there's a decision on the horizon. When he asks himself if the pain he must endure by "gutting it out" is worth the disappointment he will feel for giving up, we know what the answer will be.

The Foundations of Transformation

Adversity transforms leaders. This transformation occurs primarily because adversity and crisis generate a need for change. To some extent, leaders grow because adversity forces them to break old scripts and patterns and take new steps and new risks.

This perspective is certainly not novel. Harvard Professor John Kotter has written extensively on the process of change, particularly organizational change.[1] Kotter notes that one of the toughest challenges in leading change is to get people to move out of their comfort zone and break the patterns of the status quo. The first step in leading change is to create a clear need for change for those in the organization. But Kotter goes further to contend that there must be a "sense of urgency," a realization that without change, a crisis or critical loss will surely occur.

Kotter's notion is consistent with the psychological base of most individual change. In short, most of us are moved to change when the cost of not changing is greater than the cost of changing. Change is driven by crisis, or at least by the impending threat of crisis. Accordingly, adversity is a catalyst of change.

Second, transformation occurs because adversity forces leaders to do some soul- searching. This soul-searching may concern leadership approaches, business strategies and actions, or even the course of their lives. The search may be quick and the answers as simple as the commitment to "never do that again." Yet, the search can be deep and profound, leading to new assumptions about leadership and their roles as leaders.

It's important that crisis and adversity force leaders to dig inside themselves, question themselves, and challenge their personal assumptions. This reflective encounter can be a bit out of the ordinary and surprising. For most leaders, caught in the hectic pace of running a business and growing a career, there is little time for such reflection. This is particularly true when the needed reflection is agonizing or painful. Consequently, reflection may be resisted.

For some, adversity is an excuse to ratchet up the flurry of activity. It is a logical pattern and for most, it has worked in the past. But, transformation requires digging at the values and the heart.

We heard many stories of reflection and in-depth soul-searching. One leader noted that while a failed venture had cost the business dearly, the entire process forced him to reconsider his role and the way he dealt with people in the business. He said he learned more about himself and what was important to him than at any other time in his professional life. Another executive explained the process as a "reality check." Yet another revealed, with bold candor, the process as "digging inside myself" to try to figure out what was going on.

There is often a new sense of identity and a new focus. And, strange as it may seem, there is a new passion sparked through this reflective step. We will unfold the dynamics of this powerful step later in the book.

Third, transformation involves a reframe—a new rebound-focused attitude. Transformation is more than a cerebral process; it involves a new way of thinking, orienting, and facing reality. Many of the leaders in our study noted that rather than being depleted by adversity, they had learned to view adversity as a challenge, and were determined and motivated to respond to the challenge. Over and over we saw that successful leaders had the capacity to reframe adversity into a challenge and an opportunity.

The Adversity Cycle

Certainly we are all shaped by our experiences. Painful as it may be, we are most dramatically shaped through our struggles and experiences with adversity. To say that trials and tribulations have a dramatic, molding effect on us is certainly not novel. In *The Lessons of Experience*, a pioneering study of leadership growth and development, the authors noted that "nearly all developmental events involve a confrontation with adverse circumstances—obstacles that must be overcome."[2]

Leadership promises to contain struggles and tests. We found that successful leaders at every level of the organization face these tests, address these struggles, and through the process, learn and grow. In fact, these leaders are even bolstered and strengthened by experiences with adversity. Most of the leaders we studied indicated that good things happened as they responded to the struggles of adversity.

These leaders had experienced the struggle. They were not simply reciting cliché-ridden phrases; they were sharing a core aspect of their leader character. In short, it's one thing to say that struggle and adversity is part of leadership. It's quite another thing to experience it, to know it first hand, and to be able to accept the logic of adversity. Although easily stated, this point is so fundamental that further comment is needed.

Shaping Through Adversity—Exploring the Adversity Cycle

Successful leaders, through experience, accept adversity and recognize the powerful developmental role that adversity can play. They experience what we call the adversity cycle.

Consider the following developmental progression: First, leaders experience adversity. While never pleasant, they know it's coming, so it doesn't throw them completely off track. They persevere through the experience and, in the process, develop rebound strategies. Leaders recognize that personal growth, development, and molding of their leader character is taking place. They emerge with a new maturity and perspective and make adjustments. These responses give them the ability and confidence to handle future challenges. We found that it is precisely this maturity and confidence that enables them to step forward, courageously, and face the necessary struggles of leadership.

Three Progressive Steps

The secret to this progression lies in many areas. Successful leaders have a unique way of looking at adversity. Successful leaders view adversity through three lenses: First, they view it as an interruption. Second, they ask what was revealed through the adversity. And third, they see adversity as an opportunity for adjustment. These three views may seem rather basic, but they emerge as foundations to a healthy, transforming view of adversity. Let's look more carefully at each.

1. Adversity as Interruption. The leaders studied recognized that adversity was a necessary component of successful leadership. Though leaders do not go out looking for adversity, they accept its reality. They understand that if they execute their leadership roles properly, adversity will come. And, importantly, they understand that success is made significant through the process of adversity.

Perhaps because of these realizations, successful leaders keep mistakes, adversities, and even crises in a broad context. Leaders do not define themselves through the crisis, but by their broader pattern of success. Leaders are able to see the big picture even when an immediate problem or struggle clouds it. One leader said it succinctly, "I view adversity as an interruption." Her view was echoed by many others. This view is critical because it allows leaders to see adversity in a proper and healthy perspective. Let's explore that notion more fully.

There may be no business event that hits the crisis level as directly as the experience of being fired. As you might expect, some in our pool of leaders had encountered this unique form of adversity. Interestingly, they displayed a consistent and quite remarkable outlook toward the overall experience. They refused to be defined by the termination. They recognized that they had been successful before the firing, and they expected to be successful in the future. This termination was simply an event. Damning as it may have been, it was viewed as a temporary interruption. Even while leaders struggled with the pain, anger, and confusion of the event, they never lost perspective that this was only a blip on their record of success.

The message here is clear—adversity is an interruption, not a defining event. The crisis, the mistake, the adversity does not define character. These are simply interruptions on a path toward something more.

2. Adversity as a Revealing Event. Many people are often surprised at what is revealed during adversity and crisis. Adversity reveals what we may have attempted to keep hidden. "I really wasn't ready for that much responsibility. I hadn't learned the lessons. I should have seen it. Others saw it. My boss saw it. And I sure saw it when he demoted me." Adversity can be a harsh wake-up call, a brush with reality. In fact, it reveals and often forces one to confront that reality. The picture that is revealed is not always pretty.

Leaders are intelligent, and they are usually quick studies. So, why is there a need for a crisis wake-up call? It's built into the very structure and nature of the leader's job. Business feedback comes continually through reports and financial statements. Personal feedback is rare; what does occur is often inferred through the lens of business performance. In some cases, the need for adjustment becomes clear only after mistakes are made.

Furthermore, honest personal feedback is rare. Who provides it? No subordinate really wants to comment on the emperor's new clothes. Family and friends can be dismissed because they "really do not understand." Most leaders want to encourage supportive commentary and discourage criticism. Caught in the hectic pace of business life, many leaders simply believe they cannot stop and take the time to make needed personal adjustments. Adversity and crisis shades things differently.

The revealing quality of adversity is a unique experience for the successful leader. In some cases, it leads to a complete reexamination of what is important and what is not. For the insightful, it presents a snapshot that cannot be ignored. It forces the leader to examine and question, "What's really going on?"

Any learning, growth, and advancement that may come from adversity will be lost without a careful examination of what is revealed. The transformational nature of adversity that was noted in the previous chapter will not occur without the second lesson of adversity: Recognize what is being revealed through the adversity.

There is a caution here that must be noted, and it is one that our leaders were clear about. Leaders are action oriented. Spending time trying to figure out what is being revealed is not what they are about. Yet, this step is critical. It will not make the experience of adversity any less painful, but it will provide unexpected insight.

3. *Adversity as the Basis for Personal Adjustments.* Talking with successful leaders offered some interesting life perspectives. Many had been in leadership positions for years. In fact, most noted that they had assumed simple leadership roles early in life through sports, scouting, family ventures, and social and school activities. But all agreed that they were not the same leaders today that they were 20, 10, or even five years ago.

These leaders realized that they were not complete and finished products. They were always experiencing personal growth, development, and change. They had made a series of personal adjustments; some were small and some were large.

While personal adjustments can arise from a variety of sources, most leaders recognize the prompting impact of adversity. In other words, they change their assumptions and actions because they have to do so. In many ways, they reinforce the old counseling axiom that "we change when the pain becomes so great that we must." Adversity, disappointment, mistakes, and crisis bring leaders face to face with the reality that refusing to adjust will produce unacceptable outcomes.

The Heat of the Battle

The paradox of success and the adversity cycle make sense as you look back on your life. In retrospect, many events look different, and often they look better. Yet, does an awareness of the paradox provide much comfort when you're in the heat of battle?

The leaders we interviewed told us in clear and certain terms that the answer is "yes." While knowledge of the paradox does not mitigate the pain or distress of a serious trauma, it helps as one tries to look beyond the situation. Even in the midst of trauma, successful leaders realize that the shaping and transformation of the adversity can be good for them and their businesses. In fact, the unique self-talk that asks, "How will I feel when I beat this thing?" does occur, and is a prompting factor that drives successful leaders.

By the same token, the understanding that there is an adversity cycle permits us to approach each new trauma with more experience, perspective, and skill. This makes crises and the prospect of future adversities less daunting. People learn and develop because they recall the lessons of adversity. This is their adversity memory.

Adversity Memory

Adversity memory influences the way we confront adversity. Once you have traversed an adversity, it looks different the next time it arises. You are able to say, "I have seen this before."

The signals are more readily recognized as the events unfold. In turn, you conjure up how to respond and cope. By the same token, if you have refused to confront the elements of crisis, the lessons are tainted.

Some may argue that rebound is built solely on experience. This is shallow and even false. Rebound comes when you learn something from the experience of crisis. Experiencing a crisis without adjusting or learning from it only raises your level of fear. It encourages leaders, perhaps at a subliminal level, to do everything they can to avoid all situations that may result in crisis. Risk taking, challenge, and creativity can be thwarted in the process.

Early crises teach lessons about the adversity cycle. These painful lessons may be tucked away, but they are pulled out each time a new crisis looms.

We asked the president of a rapidly growing technology business if he could remember his first major crisis. Even before our sentence was completed, he was nodding his head. Without hesitation he vividly pinpointed the exact date the crisis broke. He noted that because of shifts in his business, he had to make some major adjustments.

These adjustments meant taking an action he swore to himself that he would never do—downsize. An entire division had to be eliminated and a number of jobs would be lost. Some of those leaving had been with the company for years and some were friends. The details in his story, retold years later, were minute, no doubt born of deep emotion. Yet, he commented that this event and his response to the event had been a prelude to subsequent experiences. Further, he noted that his pattern of response followed a fairly typical pattern—a pattern reflective of our adversity cycle.

As others retraced their experience, trauma, and process of recovery, they came to similar conclusions. What they learned from that event shaped their understanding and response to the next crisis. Each adversity added to the picture. While their approach is not yet complete, their strategies have more clarity and focus. Perhaps most important, they know they will endure and emerge because they have done so before.

The Wisdom of Experience

Adversity creates a sense of urgency, and therefore can become a catalyst for growth and change. But it can be much more. It can build character and strength. It can even transform. On the other hand, it can unravel and derail a person for life. Our actions or lack of them will determine and shape our very character.

Successful leaders, through a process of reflection, draw upon a basic set of principles and values that allow them to see adverse events in a new light. This allows them to find a way to turn adversity into a challenge. Over the years, they habituate themselves to see obstacles as opportunities. They do this because they have done it before. They have acquired, in the course of their careers, the virtues of perseverance, determination, and courage. Without these habits in place, it is doubtful that they could master their adversities. It is this combination of thinking and virtue that allows them to find a way to turn adversity into a challenge.

Our leaders viewed adversity as part of the natural course of events in business and in life. They experienced it as a source of feedback, often unpleasant, about themselves and their behavior. It provided them an opportunity to take corrective action.

In the end, adversity was turned into an opportunity for personal and professional growth that left them with a sense of enhanced competence. They seemed to have developed a philosophy of life that had as one of its tenants: What does not destroy me only makes me stronger.

PART

III

NO MAN
IS AN ISLAND

8

Rebound Networks

"Without friends, you really have no life."

One of the most personal and honest interviews we conducted took place over lunch in a conference room adjacent to the president's office. With business buzzing around us, he revealed the personal impact of business adversity with clarity, passion, and depth. More importantly, though, he talked of the support that helped him persevere and rebound.

"When I get particularly discouraged about [the business], my wife reminds me about how good our relationship is and the relationships with our girls—and that is really success enough. The ability to go home and not have a bunch of issues to deal with has made the difficulties of business much easier to deal with. Of course, I attribute much of that to her. But there are things I did. I never got involved with playing golf and those kinds of things, because I spent time with the family. At that time [in the midst of a business adversity], I could only do two things. I could do the family and the business, and that's about it."

He spoke in open terms about some of the pressing business problems he had faced. Some seemed consuming, even overwhelming. We looked for the secret to his resilience—his rebound. He noted that adversity had drawn him into a deeper faith relationship with God. He focused less on the adversities and failures and more on how he could grow and mature through these experiences.

He spoke of his business and the core values that defined the culture of his business: "I guess it boils down to core values—integrity, service, excellence, and community. We feel like we are being successful if we are performing for our customers and for each other with integrity; if we are serving them with excellence." He explained further, "I will often sacrifice … to do the right thing."

In the next few chapters, we will explore, in depth, what leaders experience when they are confronted with adversity. The emotions and reactions will appear familiar. You will be struck by the pattern of similarity between these stories of leadership and your personal story.

Of course, our goal is not simply to describe an experience. We want to describe the path through the experience. We want to share with you a path that progresses from adversity to eventual challenge and success. This is the rebound path.

Along the rebound path are the burning questions that each of us know all too well. If you are in the midst of crisis right now, these questions are consuming your thoughts and energies: Will I survive? How can I make sense of this? What do I need to do? How can I move past this? How can I survive? Where do I turn?

That last question may be one of the most revealing. Where do you turn? Whose advice do you follow? Some may choose to "go it alone." As you will see, there is a time and place for serious introspection. More importantly, you will see that successful leaders have well-defined and carefully developed rebound networks that serve to facilitate the rebound journey.

The leader in the opening vignette to this chapter recognized the value of these networks. He realized that being a strong, skilled, and hard working executive was not enough. He drew upon his rebound network. His wife, his family, and his faith complemented and enhanced his personal strength and dedication.

This chapter looks at the possible rebound networks available to leaders. We will discuss how each of these network sources can help. We will then see their roles unfold more fully as we look at the leader rebound through the remainder of the book. Keep in mind that these networks are sources that we draw upon to help us work through, figure out, and respond to the questions and challenges of adversity.

The Internal Rebound Network: Self-Reliance

Leaders are a self-reliant group of people. Successful leaders believe that they affect their own outcomes more than anyone or anything else. Their experiences and successes have born this out. They have succeeded through hard work, dedication, and the ability to stay focused. They have framed a broad plan, but they have also taken care of the details.

We saw this inner focus when we asked our leader participants to summarize values and offer words of insight for younger managers to consider. Consistently, they emphasized hard work, persistence, and passion. These leaders understood that random events occur. Sometimes you get lucky, and sometimes fate seems to turn against you. Yet, they understood that hard work and steady commitment could handle a sea of unforeseen and unpredictable twists on the path of leadership.

Further, these leaders knew that random events, luck, fate, or chance usually do not make the difference. Accordingly, when adversity appeared, leaders saw themselves, first and foremost, as the source for working through the troubles. Listen to their language: "I don't let myself get down. A defeatist attitude is contagious. There's no place in business for that type of an attitude." "Have a goal, work hard, have fun, and always give more than you get. If you do all those things, you're going to be successful." There is fundamental logic behind this view. Research suggests that effective leaders are self-confident.[1] There is also evidence that leaders who are more effective under conditions of adversity have an internal locus of control.[2]

This term "control" is often overstated and misunderstood. It does not suggest that effective leaders believe they have complete control over all adversity, such thinking would be little more than folly. Those with an internal locus of control believe that they have enough control over their lives and circumstances that they can work things out, perform, and succeed. However, these findings do not mean that successful leaders will not use or rely on others. Quite the contrary. Part of these leaders' personal ability to cope is due to the manner in which they use their rebound networks.

This point is tricky. It smacks of a rugged individualism that can be taken too far. Accordingly, we need to be careful and present a critical caveat. The image of rugged individualism, standing

71

straight and tall in the face of trouble, is well ingrained. The myth goes like this: When adversity comes, leaders toughen up and take it. When crisis strikes, they step up and deal with it. Strong, resilient, and fearless, the leader "goes it alone."

This Rambo-like image of leadership under adversity is dangerous. It's a myth that was probably never true, and today it makes little sense at all. Resilient, rebound leaders rarely "go it alone." They recognize that there is no weakness in drawing on others for help and support. In fact, the development and use of others—those rebound networks—becomes a key to a leader's ability to bounce back from adversity. Successful leaders understand, develop, and use external rebound networks.

External Rebound Networks

Rebound networks affect leaders in three ways. First, these networks offer emotional support. Support networks listen and provide genuine concern for the leader. The network encourages and bolsters the leader, enhancing the leader's confidence that they can overcome the adversity.[3] Indeed, numerous studies have reported that social support reduces the psychological impact of stress.[4] Notice the strong support that the leader in our opening example received.

Appropriate emotional support builds and enhances rather than pities. Significantly, we encountered no incidence of what some have called regressive coping.[5] Regressive coping occurs when the support network facilitates self-pitying leader behavior. In regressive coping, support networks encourage and even add to the leaders' tendency to see life's events as an unfortunate and unfair series of actions conspiring against the leader. This breeds an attitude of victimization. Research suggests that such regressive support diminishes rather than enhances resilience and rebound.[6] Again, we did not see this form of action from the support base of our study. Typical of our findings was the response of one leader who spoke of his wife, "She is supportive and it's so important. (She) wouldn't let me wallow in self-pity."

Second, support networks offer diversionary support. Here, the networks serve as an escape from the rigors of adversity. The networks help take the leader's mind away from the elements and trauma of adversity. They allow the leader to be involved in meaningful activity rather than focusing on adversity. In the process, they help the leader relax and strengthen the leader's capacity to respond to adversity in the future. Evidence suggests that those involved in such meaningful diversionary activities experience better mental health and less psychological distress.[7] This diversionary function also helps the leader see the bigger picture of life and view events in a more reasonable framework of overall importance. In short, diversionary support helps leaders place the adversity in perspective.

Third, support networks offer good, sound advice, thereby playing an advisory support role. Here, the networks offer input and information that help the leader understand and cope with the adversity. That advice may be quite specific: "You have to deal with that person now." Or the advice may be more general: "Give it some time. See what shakes out. It may not be as bad as you think." In any case, the advisory role offers insight and guidance that the leader can use during the adversity struggle.

Family

Our findings in the family area are not surprising, and the intensity of the comments are strong and consistent. When asked to explain how family had affected their careers, participants generally noted the positive impact of family. "If I didn't have family backing, I don't think I'd be where I am today. I mean it would be more of a struggle. I am very fortunate that my family has been behind me and supported the decisions I had to make."

This positive impact is seen in two key family roles, each affecting the leader's ability to rebound. First, family is a source of emotional support and encouragement. A number of participants noted that their spouse understood the career demands and provided the support necessary to continue a consuming work schedule.

Second, family provides a solace and refuge from the rigors and demands of the work world. Here, family plays a diversionary role. The family mediates or serves to buffer the leader from the full impact of adversity. This effect, consistent with what we encounter in stress literature, lessens the psychological effects of adversity. One participating leader even noted that the family was "the best health club in the world."

While family may play an advisory role, our study shows that, in most cases, family gives only the broadest and most general advice. Family impact is far more important for its emotional support and diversionary roles.

Most of the leaders interviewed took steps to spend time with their families. Leaders noted a variety of techniques to balance work and family demands. Some leaders arrived at work very early so they could spend time with their children at night. Many did additional work after the family had gone to bed for the evening.

Some tried to segment work and family time. "We don't discuss work at home." "Before I leave my desk [at night] I write down on a 3 X 5 card those things I need to do tomorrow. . . . Last thing I do is organize all the little notes and leave it right here [on my desk]. When I come in the morning, I just pick it up." Many felt such techniques allowed the family time to be a break from the regular business demands. Additionally, it was a fair and considerate way to treat the family.

However, others brought the issues and stresses of work home and shared their personal frustrations with their family. For example, the leader in our opening vignette felt comfortable taking this approach. Those in this camp recognize that open communication is at the heart of a successful marriage and meaningful family experiences. They suggested that a refusal to discuss work—the area of life that demanded their greatest focus—would be a serious breach of communication. "You can share everything. Nothing is held back. Your happiness and sorrow, the good times and bad, get shared and help you maintain a good perspective."

One leader commented that his entire family ate dinner together as often as they could. "No one has ever spoken it, but we all know that dinner is a very important time. And we all have taken the view that we will spend one to two hours at the dinner table. We don't eat in the kitchen. [We] use the good china, candles on the table. Every meal is recognized as important. They [his family] wait for me, and we try to go over the events of the day. Everybody talks about their day."

Different approaches work for different people. There is certainly value and merit in both of the approaches noted above. Our evidence indicates that leaders who use the sharing model realize rebound advantages. However, the ability to "escape in the family" also serves as a rebound buffer. So how should the leader approach the family?

First, leaders do need to share. Those who fail to do so wear a mask of solitude. The leader may even reason that he or she will weather the storms of the day, return home stoically, and keep the family from the traumas of the work world. Such thinking is largely bunk. Most leaders still bring it home. It's read in their tension, withdrawn nature, or even open anger. They just don't talk about it.

However, at some point, after issues have been discussed, the leader must move from these issues and address other family matters. In this manner, the family can truly serve its diversionary role. For most leaders, the search for work and family balance is quite demanding. The leaders in our study practiced numerous techniques and approaches to achieve this balance. For example, a number of leaders attempted to make sure that at least some business trips were also family trips, thereby promoting closer family contacts and providing wonderful learning and growth opportunities for the children.

Unfortunately, the harsh reality was that the leaders had done a poor job of balancing work and family. Many noted, in retrospective resignation, that they had devoted so much time and energy to the business that they had not achieved an appropriate or desirable balance. In general, the group saw this as a trade-off.

Few participants felt that family had any detrimental effect on their careers. Rather, the family played a significant role in making them feel successful. In fact, when asked if they could redo some aspect of their life, our leaders said they would find a way to carve out more time for their family.

Friendships

Generally, the network of close friends was quite small. In most cases, these friendships spanned a number of years and often began because of similarity of interests. Frequently, children or similar family values drew leaders into friendships. In most cases, these friendships were unrelated to the business or career context. With few exceptions, the closest friendships tended to be outside the organization.

A significant minority of leaders even reported no close friends. Further, a significant minority reported their spouse as being their best friend. A number of respondents noted that the lack of friends was a regret, particularly at their current stage in life. They could see value in having an extended or deeper set of close friends. However, they noted that in many cases they simply did not have the time to devote to developing and maintaining the contacts necessary to build close friendships. This, too, was a trade-off. Simply stated, working long hours and spending spare time with the family left little time to form close friendships.

Close friendships affect the leader's rebound indirectly by providing a pressure-free escape from the regular demands and challenges of the career. Close friendships provide the same support, escape, and rejuvenation as the family, though to a lesser extent. However, the largest role of close friendships seems to be as a diversion. "I rarely talk to my close friends about business . . . I always figure people don't really care about my problems . . . So I think it's time for people to meet in the middle and relax. Just enjoy each others' company, play golf, go out for dinner, whatever."

Of course, there are issues of propriety here. Leaders are aware that in order to maintain confidentiality and treat employees with proper respect, they have to be careful about what is said about the business and the people involved. Sharing details of a business adversity may be unwise, even among close friends.

To some extent, close friendships help provide perspective and help build the leader up during adversity. As one leader commented about his closest friends, "They'll make comments. You know, remember you've got a tremendous family. You've been very successful. Remember what hardship could be." He went on to note that such friendships had a way of jolting him during adversity. Friends "get you out of the issues of feeling sorry for yourself and getting you into the ability of feeling pretty good about what you have been able to do." Another leader commented that his close friends knew nothing about his business but added that the friends were "assets to the soul."

Importantly, the role of close friends shifts when the adversity goes from the business to the personal realm. When family problems or personal problems arise, these friendships play an important emotional support role.

Peers

Peer networks are associates who understand and have experience that may be helpful in confronting and dealing with adversity. In some cases, these peers are from the same organization as the leader. Here, the leader can turn to a trusted colleague for help or guidance. More often, peer networks are comprised of leaders and managers from other organizations. They are business acquaintances who come together to pursue some common goals. The networks can be quite informal, such as calling a leader friend for lunch. However, they can be more highly formalized. For example, some leaders belong to a leadership council, where they meet and share with small groups of leaders. Typically, these leaders are not from competing industries, and discussions are held in the strictest confidence. Others belong to broader networks, such as the Young Presidents Organization (YPO).

These networks are significant because they are made up of people who can relate to what the leader is experiencing. Therefore, peer networks function as sounding boards. Further, peer networks offer both emotional support and meaningful advice.

We found rebound leaders tend to network with other rebound people. Some even go so far as to say that if peers focused on negative thinking or pessimistic views, the leaders stopped associating with them.

Spirituality

Respondents were asked what spirituality meant to them and their lives. Additionally, they were asked how spirituality affected their careers. This facet, while highly personal, produced careful and reflective responses. Nearly all of the leaders experienced some sense of spirituality. For example, nearly all recognized that one's life and work is a small piece of a bigger picture. Four views of spirituality emerged.

First, some likened spirituality to organized religion and admitted to having no close connection or commitment to any organized religious focus. This group was quite small.

Second, some demonstrated no outward evidence of spiritual connection or practice, such as a church affiliation. However, they viewed themselves as deeply spiritual.

Third, some likened spirituality to a personal philosophy or dogma regarding the significance and role of people and how they should be treated. In this regard, most expressed a well-defined sense of values, noting that these were consistent with the prevailing value themes of most organized religions.

Fourth, some expressed a deep, abiding, and personal faith that affected their lives and their careers. This group, by and large, drew upon some form of organized religion. They viewed their personal faith as both a compass for direction and as a basis of measurement. About a third of the leaders we studied fell into this category.

For this fourth group, their faith carried both emotional support and advisory roles. Some studies, such as the classic work of Laura Nash, have noted that people frequently adopt two personalities or identities—a private religious identity and a career identity.[8] This certainly was not the case with this fourth group. Their business lives were direct and logical extensions of their spiritual lives.

Many leaders believed that the answers and approaches to their toughest adversities lay in spiritual truths. While difficult to express and define, the intensity of belief was glaring. "There is no doubt in my mind that without God I would not have gotten to where I am today. I think He has helped me. I think He has put me in the right place at the right time . . . I don't know what His plan is, but I've got to keep doing what I have to keep doing, and if I do that, then it's going to be okay . . . I look back and there are too many times in my life that I think—yeah it looks like a coincidence, and it wasn't. That was God. He did that. I know it. There's not a doubt in my mind."

Speaking of the trials of adversity, another leader added, "I'd be perfectly willing to be done with [a business crisis], for these trials to be over. But, I dealt with it . . . by spending time in God's word and spending time with Him . . . I don't think there's a separation between the sacred and the secular."

There was a consistent theme among this group: Adversities helped them draw closer to their God and experience a growing depth of faith. Others noted that their faith helped when they experienced the grip of fear. "I try not to worry about what I can't control. I put it in God's hands." Some went even further, commenting that they were not sure they could have endured the perils of adversity without their faith foundations.

A number of leaders noted that their faith achieved a deeper personal dimension through the searching process prompted by adversity. The words of one dynamic and highly successful leader were typical of other leaders who turned to their faith: "I believe in God, and I have a deep spiritual sense. This gives me great inner strength." For this group, reflection and introspection were naturally linked in their minds with their personal faith journey.

Nearly all respondents noted that spiritually and faith provide a base of values and principles that helps them focus and discover their foundations as they grapple with adversity. The values noted were fairly consistent and were similar to those identified in previous studies.[9] One leader commented that faith provides a set of values, even some absolutes, which guides the way people are treated and business is done. Another noted that faith provides principles that permeate career and life. In general, our leaders spoke of the illogical sense that beliefs and principles can be compartmentalized. They cannot, and the principles should not be compromised. One leader commented, quite colorfully, that "spirituality provides both a compass for setting your direction and a yardstick for measuring that the values of faith are put into action."

Honesty and integrity were the most frequently mentioned values followed by adhering to high ethical standards and principles. The next most frequently mentioned value set had to do with being open and straightforward. Instilling a culture of mutual respect, demonstrating persistence, and practicing sincerity were noted commonly. More than one third of the respondents noted that their personal values were really restatements of Judeo-Christian values, stemming from their religious foundations.

Balance

In order to experience the leader rebound, a network of rebound support must be present. While successful leaders often adhere to an ethic of rugged individualism, they have learned through experience that this is an insufficient base when confronted with challenging adversity and crisis. Accordingly, successful leaders strive to nourish and develop their bases of support. In simplest terms, there seems little doubt that leaders who have a balanced network of support are better able to weather adversity and express a successful rebound.

This balance of self-reliance and external support is often trying and at times even counter intuitive. Confronted with crisis, many leaders tend to pull away from family, friends, and peers. Our research has shown the value of moving beyond this natural tendency. This study emphasizes the powerful and positive role that support networks hold. While the specific networks differed somewhat from leader to leader, all those we interviewed had learned the value of external support.

Young and emerging leaders must realize that there is no argument that talent and hard work are indispensable qualities for leader success. Yet, in the pit of adversity, they are rarely sufficient. We encourage those of you at the early stages of leadership to carefully cultivate strong and supportive rebound networks.

As we progress through the remaining chapters, you will see the impact of rebound networks in the context of the overall adversity and rebound process. You will also have the opportunity to explore your personal rebound networks to a greater extent.

The Wisdom of Experience

To go through adversity well we need assistance. Only an arrogant person thinks and acts as if he or she is self–sufficient. The sources of emotional support and counsel are derived from friends, family, God, peers, consultants, etc. We have labeled these "rebound networks." The wise leader knows when and how to call upon them. Successful leaders draw upon their rebound networks for the emotional support and advice they need to weather the storm. They know that "no man is an island" and that a healthy self-reliance means knowing how and when to seek assistance.

It is clear that different kinds of support are needed during the various phases of a crisis. There is a time for plain emotional release and support. At other times, diversionary support is required. Family and friends, more often than not, provide this type of support. Yet, this is not the time for concrete advice. The peer network seems to a primary source of advice, although peers can provide emotional support also. In the end, all of this prepares the individual to be receptive to advice from the appropriate rebound network.

PART IV

A JOURNEY DISRUPTED

9

The Great Disruption

"At the time it was devastating!"

I have fired a lot of people. I was always a little curious about why people got so bent out of shape about it. It was business. And I applied my own definitions—it was a business decision! However, well, when I got fired, it was business also. But it wasn't to me. I didn't realize how personal and traumatic that is to an individual until it happened to me! At the time it was devastating."

Life disruptions are inevitable. The question is not how to avoid them, but how to manage them when they arrive. Now, it is true that just as we can make our own luck we can also create our own misfortunes. For the moment we will assume that most managers do the best they can with the information they have and within the context in which they work. We are not discussing those who are hobbled with self-destructive habits.

Some disruptions occur without notice while others are anticipated. Like the CEO quoted above, surprise is the typical reaction for those sudden and unforeseen big events. But since we are talking about adverse events that threaten personal and organization equilibrium, shock is the more descriptive word. Shock disorients, confuses, and puzzles. One loses clarity of thought and direction for a period of time. And at the biological level, a state of arousal occurs. The entire immune system can be affected.

The majority of us will never be fired, declare bankruptcy, be held hostage, suffer from life-threatening cancer, or face other threatening disasters. Yet all human beings have similar reactions to shocking events, even though they may not show it in their behavior. Disruptions and subsequent reactions are experienced in degrees. They may be short or long-lived, but from the extreme cases we learn how the process of disruption is best handled.

Let's return to the fired CEO. He continued, "On the evening I got fired, people came over to spend time with me—a whole yard full—and I broke down. And it was good to get some of it out. But in the next week or two, after all the phone calls came in, all of which happened in a couple of days, then it got pretty lonely. And I'll tell you how I dealt with it. Well, it evolved. It didn't just happen. I didn't wake up one morning and say, 'ah-ha, here's the solution.'"

He talked about the initial confusion associated with shock. "I was very crazy. This is about the best word I can think of to define the first few days. I did some things that were just, in retrospect, very strange. Every day, after working-out for about an hour and a half or so (I got in great shape physically), I would go into my office and go over my finances. I would line up all my assets and all my liabilities, and all of everything else. That makes a lot of sense, but should you do that every day? I mean, every day!"

"Look, not much changes in 24 hours when you're not working, but I had to do it. It was compulsive behavior. When I finally got through just reassuring myself that I could go for a couple of years without a paycheck—I've always lived below my income—and still make it, I decided that I wasn't interested in taking another job. Yet I had a lot of really negative, really, really, seriously negative thoughts."

Shock, that initial disrupting event, has a tendency to sever or loosen us from our anchors of stability, either personal or professional. A period of confusion ensues. "I can't figure out why it happened" is a typical response to this stage of disruption. We seem to think that if we know why it happened, we can reverse events or find a clear path of action. But shocking events can't be reversed, and there is no clear path of action. We have conceptualized the initial phase of the rebound as disillusionment.

Denial and fear surround the phase of disillusionment. Denial takes many forms from "this can't be true" to "it's not all that bad." Denial is one mechanism that is used to manage our confusion about what should be done. Others manage confusion by repetitively reviewing and analyzing why it happened.

Fear is manifested through disappointment, embarrassment, hopelessness, loss of energy, and feelings of failure and inadequacy. Of course, there is also the blackness of depression that can envelop a person. Everyone experiences some degree of fear and denial. If not managed well, they can become overwhelming and immobilizing. Some careers end up on these rocks.

The second phase of the rebound is reflection. This phase of recovery often includes anger. The mix of feelings experienced in the first phase usually consolidates into anger. If properly expressed, this is a healthy step. The person is in touch with energy—the kind of psychic energy that will be needed to overcome adversity. But anger must be transformed into creative action.

The way our fired CEO transformed his anger into creative action is very typical of a positive recovery process. "I was thinking about the 'unfair' way I had been treated, and all that; and it was dragging me down. So I sat there one day, and began thinking about all this, and I thought: 'You know, I've got 100 percent of my energy.' Everybody has 100 percent of what they have, and right now, I was spending 80 percent of it being bitter, frustrated, and angry, and all these other emotions. Well, that's not me. That's not an upbeat person—a fun person. And that's not the way I wanted to be."

"So, I thought, you know, I can sit here and I can turn into somebody I'm not, and I can become a bitter, ruthless person; or, I can use as much of that 100 percent energy that I have in a positive direction. So, from that point on, I started trying to minimize the amount of energy I spent on negative thoughts; and I'm not going to tell you that I went from 80 percent negative to zero.

"I'm not at zero today. I don't think about it much, but when I do, I allow myself every now and then to think about what bitter, angry, and resentful people look like. Now, I don't want to be that kind of person. All in all, I really think I cut this kind of thinking to 20 percent, which is still a huge amount of energy expended on negative things, but it's a hell of an improvement from where I was."

This process takes time and even then the emotional reactions to a great disruption usually linger. It can last from hours to months, depending upon the depth of the disruption. Crises where business, career, or personal survival is threatened, will likely take longer than more common inconveniences or missteps.

The CEO noted, "Probably, the change started within a couple of weeks, but it probably took, oh, a month or two before I was back to some semblance of normality. Within a couple of months I was able to control it well enough that other people couldn't tell. And within three or four months, it wasn't an issue. Nevertheless, every now and then you backslide a little bit, and you think, geez, what could I have done differently and all that kind of stuff, and you realize 'oh this is goofy.' So, looking back, it went rather quickly. At the time, it seemed forever."

The final phase in the rebound process, adjustment, involves not only accepting reality, but also reframing the entire event. How an individual thinks about the matter is central to a successful rebound. Determination to move on and make the most of the disruption is a sign that the leader has arrived at the last stage of the rebound process.

The CEO concludes by saying: "I wasn't going to be driven out of town because I got fired. So I took it then as a challenge, and turned it to a positive rather than a negative event. In retrospect, it was a wonderful thing that happened, because it gave me the opportunity to do a real check of my value system and my standards, and various relationships in the family and outside the family, and we all stood the test of time and I think it made me a better person. It surely made me a lot more compassionate."

This story paints in relief the critical phases associated with a successful rebound from a great disruption. The leader must pass through a set psychological process to constructively adjust to the disruption. If one step is bypassed the disruption will come back and haunt.

The great disruption creates shock and confusion. This is followed by a phase of fear and denial. This is a period when the pain from the blow is being absorbed psychologically and physically. It is the recognition that this really hurt in so many ways. It is the moment when every sense of competence and worth is threatened. Depression and a sense of loss dominate.

A period of anger follows. Anger is a form of energy. Like all energy it can be used for constructive as well as destructive purposes. Anger counters the initial depressive effects of the disruption's assault on the self. The challenge is to harness this energy for constructive, even creative purposes.

Finally, the leader emerges into the reframing and redirecting stage of the rebound. This is the period when the event is no longer seen as devastating or as a set-back, but as a challenge or an opportunity to improve.

A Choice of Paths

While all experience a similar initial reaction to adversity, all do not choose the same paths of response. This choice of paths is the difference between rebound and destruction.

As we have described, the great disruption of adversity shocks the system. Natural feelings of confusion and uncertainty ensue. Fear and denial follow, with a barrage of frustration, disappointment, embarrassment, and worry. Anger sets in.

It is in this stage of anger, under the tug of this powerful emotional mover, that the leader must make a choice. The response to anger can debilitate and destroy, leading to a surrender of hope. Or, the response to anger can be one of reformation and transformation, the very heart of rebound.

Those who choose the destructive path become resentful and bitter. They feel negative and depleted. Their spirit is bruised. They carry their resentment; their anger remains and intensifies. They bring their anger with them to new situations. From their point of view, life's events are conspiring against them. They become vindictive. The weight of adversity has crushed them. They emerge with a scarred and tainted view of life.

You know these people. Privately, you may even admit that you are or have been one of them. The reasons for their choices may make sense. We do not seek to minimize or trivialize the crises that may have prompted them to move down this path.

A few years ago, we encountered a manager barely clinging to organizational life. A promising corporate climber only five years earlier, this man, now only 40, was one step from dismissal. Not only had his performance slid to unacceptable levels, but he met all organizational attempts at correction with half-hearted responses and further decline. Beyond his personal performance, he had become a toxic presence, spreading his anger and negativism to those around him. Peers would lobby to be sure he was not assigned to one of their projects or teams.

A mystery? Not really. Nearly everyone knew and understood why. They empathized and admitted they weren't sure that their behavior, if faced with similar events, would have been different. Each could pinpoint the moment of decline: five years earlier, his only child had contracted a rare form of cancer and within months had died. Devastating, unbelievable, and unfair? Of course. But five years later, he was literally being given his last chance to salvage a career.

Rebound leaders face crises, and they take a different turn. They reframe adversity. Adversity changes them; they, too, are transformed, never to be quite the same. The lessons of adversity are still wrenching, painful, and heartfelt. But, they somehow take a different path.

Thirty-five leaders told us stories of adversity. They shared the confusion, uncertainty, fear, and even some of the anger. Some even admitted to beginning the venture down the path of destruction, and some even stayed there a while. But these successful leaders sooner or later took a turn, and they began the journey along the rebound path. The path has definite markers leading to challenge, courage, and success. As you turn to read the next chapter, we will begin to unfold that path and that journey. It is the adversity challenge.

───────────── *The Wisdom of Experience* ─────────────

In this chapter, we have introduced the psychological dynamics associated with a major disruption in the life of the leader. We have taken the extreme example of being fired as a way of illustrating the three-fold process that is an integral part of a rebound from adversity.

Disillusionment is the initial state of the rebound process and successful leaders recognize that this is an inevitable event in the course of their career. Nevertheless, this phase is marked by confusion and loss of control.

The second phase, reflection, is characterized by anger and determination. This source of energy can be used creatively to mobilize oneself to turn obstacles into advantages. Anger can also by used destructively to incriminate others and oneself and to bathe in resentment. Reflection is also a period of entertaining various courses of action and a time when one is open to advice and counsel.

The third phase, adjustment, is where a final reframing of the adverse event occurs. The trick here is to conceptualize both the event and one's life in the context in which it occurred. What was first experienced as an obstacle is now viewed as an opportunity and a challenge. A course of action is set and the leader moves on.

THE PATH
THROUGH ADVERSITY–
INSIGHT

10

The Rebound Process: Disillusionment

"I was in shock. I was numb… I was on auto-pilot."

Dee was energetic, talented, and ready. She was in her early 40's, armed with an MBA, and a solid track record in various assignments. She expected the vacant vice presidency would be hers. The promotion made sense. She had taken on some tough assignments, including her most recent two-year stint leading an area of the business that had been a clear trouble spot. She rose to the challenge. She made some tough calls, and she probably ruffled a few feathers in the process. But she got results. The bottom line displayed her score with winning clarity. The turnaround had been a success, far in excess of what had been anticipated. Friday's corporate announcement would move her one notch closer to eventually leading the company. She knew, and even admitted to those closest to her, that her time had come. But she was wrong!

Confusion

When we met, nearly two weeks after the fateful Friday, she was confused. Her questions were overwhelming. She wondered if she had pushed too hard during the turnaround. Had she offended the wrong people? Was her take-charge style too aggressive? Or did people feel she just didn't have the right stuff to cut it at the next level? Was she simply blind to her shortcomings? Had she missed some of the political signals? Was she caught in a power play beyond her grasp? She was puzzled and had been locked in the throes of an emotionally draining search for the past two weeks. She needed answers. She needed to get her hands around the situation. She still hadn't figured out how.

Disillusionment

In a book that speaks of resiliency and rebound, it may appear ironic to discuss how the typical initial response to adversity is disillusionment. But we want to look at what actually happens, what is experienced, and how changes are carried out. The leaders we interviewed described a path out of the pit of adversity and crisis. That path promises transformation and personal growth. And the path starts here, with disillusionment.

Dee was experiencing it as we spoke. She was struggling with disillusionment. She sought comfort, and she sought advice. She searched to find personal understanding. She looked for significance and meaning. Her search was neither easy nor pleasant.

Disillusionment is a period of uncertainty. It carries with it a numbing effect and a gnawing emptiness. There is confusion, despair, a temporary lack of assurance, strain, stress, and often a sense of desperation. Leaders find themselves under a rush of feelings. One leader described this initial period by saying that "it hurts." Another commented that things are "very crazy" during this period. Disillusionment may shock the individual leader. In fact, one of the leaders in our study described his personal crisis exactly this way: "I was in shock. I was numb. All perspective had suddenly changed. I was on auto-pilot."

Accepting Disillusionment

Successful leaders do not deny the presence of disillusionment. Instead, they realize that some initial down period is to be expected. The leaders we interviewed spoke openly and honestly about their emotions during this time of disillusionment. Though they felt fear, frustration, confusion, and disappointment, the leaders did not run from these emotions.

We want to emphasize two themes. First, disillusionment is a natural reaction to adversity or crisis. It has nothing to do with one's intelligence, character, position, or past accomplishments. It has everything to do with the disruptive nature of adversity. It is important to realize that feeling disillusioned is not a sign of weakness. It signals sanity and health. In fact, we may wonder about the makeup of a leader who hits adversity without some period of frustration, anxiety, or even brief depression.

One organization we worked with faced particularly challenging events. We first encountered a group of their managers after a major downsizing. These managers exhibited many of the classic signs of the survivor syndrome—guilt, confusion, and a sense that all logical fairness had been breached. Over time, these emotions subsided. Less than a year later, another round of downsizing occurred, and again the same emotions rose. Six months later, amid rampant rumors of a takeover of the business, these same emotions pressed forward once more. These were good and valued managers. They were, for the most part, successful. Regardless of how the business spun, they knew that they would continue to be successes. Yet, the emotions of disillusionment resurfaced again and again in the face of adversity.

This leads to the second theme emphasized by the leaders we studied. Our leaders recognized that disillusionment is commonly felt. Realizing it sweeps over everyone who faces adversity, our leaders did not fear this emotion. Here, the leaders' responses were revealing. One leader commented that she "wasn't sure what was going on," but, she noted, "I've felt this before. It's a sense of disappointment and uncertainty. It's like all sorts of emotional signals are going off." She added that she knew these feelings were natural and even expected. She even knew that they would eventually pass. Her perspective here is important. She was not overly bothered by the emotions. She saw no reason to pretend they did not exist. The emotions were accepted for what they were and nothing more.

Our leaders were able to accept disillusionment because they had encountered the feelings and emotions of this stage before. Because these feelings were accepted as a natural part of the adversity experience, there was neither unwarranted concern nor a lapse into deeper depression.

Three Strategies for Disillusionment

The choice of terms here is important. One does not just "get through" disillusionment. Successful leaders, through their actions, "work through" their disillusionment. They move through this period and attempt to do so quickly.

Sometimes, this process looks a bit cut and dried. One leader commented, in a rather matter–of–fact manner, "I get frustrated, express my feelings, get it all out—then it's gone and done." The overall description of this process may be accurate, but the activities involved are much more complex.

What are the key steps or strategies for handling this period of disillusionment? In this chapter, we will explore three fundamental strategies: cognitive controls, emotional controls, and behavioral controls. Cognitive controls force leaders to place adversity experiences into a proper overall perspective. This can be difficult because adversity and crisis carry a powerful emotional force that can obscure the big picture. Leaders use emotional controls to keep their feelings in check so the pangs of disillusionment don't overwhelm them and then plunge them into a debilitating emotional low. Emotional control grows through the aid of a strong network of support, particularly from family and friends. Behavioral controls deal with projecting an outer image of control in the midst of internal confusion and uncertainty. This strategy projects steady and assuring signals to the leader's business contacts.

1. The Big Picture: Cognitive Controls. First, successful leaders keep in mind the big picture. Consistent with our earlier points, they understand that adversity is merely an interruption and not a definition of who they are. The leaders said it well: "When I hit the low point, I realize that (these) things are always temporary." Another went back to an old adage and philosophy, noting that he always tried to keep in mind that "this too shall pass." These leaders grasped, even in the midst of despair, that they are successes. They employed a coping technique known as cognitive controls.

True, they may not have felt like successes at this particular low point, but experience had taught them that there would be a brighter future. One leader spoke to this theme clearly and cleverly. "The brightest guy in the world can study something and still make a poor decision because he didn't turn over the right rock. And the dumbest guy can make a great decision because he just got lucky. I prepare but I don't dwell on the negatives."

2. Don't Get Too Low: Emotional Controls. Next, successful leaders don't let themselves get too low. Leaders are quite cognizant of the need to avoid wallowing in self-pity. "You create your own atmosphere. If you allow yourself to be negative, it draws you in and sucks you down."

Successful leaders demonstrate a keen awareness that to languish in disillusionment —to remain in that state too long—is dangerous. Either from personal experience or from observation, they grasp a fundamental psychological principle: disillusionment can grow and lead to bitterness, anger, and eventual depression. Even in the midst of disillusionment, they consistently note a key rebound theme: "You can't let yourself get too low."

Jeanie Duck, in her insightful thoughts on managing change, offers a memorable image. She comments that it's OK to visit Pity City, you just can't move in.[1] Successful leaders understand this distinction. They also seem to be aware of the signals that their residency is shifting to Pity City. For example, one leader noted that he tended to withdraw when he became disillusioned. When he saw this occurring, he realized that he needed to move forward. Another noted that he would become highly critical of those closest to him, particularly family members. When this pattern began to unfold, he knew he'd languished too long in disillusionment. Another leader told a powerful story of his mounting frustration and disappointment until his wife provided the critical wake-up call, "You're not a very happy person to be around anymore."

Successful leaders avoid doing certain things during the disillusionment period. They do not fall into the "why me" syndrome. Naturally, those experiencing adversity may have a tendency to say, "Why is this happening to me?" or "What did I do to deserve this?" or "Why are these things coming together like this?" Such reactions would be common conclusions given the basic unfairness of many adversities. But the leaders interviewed, with overwhelming consistency, did not take that stance. Rather, they said, "Why not me?" They seemed to accept that adversity spares no one. Accordingly, they were able to avoid many of the traps of unnecessary self-pity. This helped them from getting too low.

Leaders found other ways to keep themselves from getting too low. Commonly, they moved toward diversionary activity with family or friends. During disillusionment support networks become very important. However, let's note a key point. The purpose of a support network during this stage is not to provide answers to the issues and problems. The leader is not yet ready for answers. During disillusionment, support networks exist so leaders have someone to talk to. They provide the emotional support we discussed in the last chapter. The network helps leaders define who they are and helps leaders put the adverse events in perspective. Support networks may play the role of being a sounding board. But most important, these networks are there when leaders need to talk.

Let's emphasize the significance of this point more fully. Leaders need to talk through their feelings of disillusionment. Again, the myth of rugged individualism fights against this fundamental need. Many leaders have a mistaken concept that the emotions of disillusionment must be suppressed rather than expressed. However, suppressed emotions do not go away. They merely seethe beneath the surface. They usually come out, often at inopportune times as additional stress is encountered. Suppressed emotions breed anger and resentment.

The rule here is simple. Leaders should express their emotions in an appropriate forum. In reality, most people can move through the period of disillusionment more quickly if they have a chance to talk about it. The question becomes, to whom do you turn?

Leaders see a need to shield the business or at least most of the people in the business from this emotive period, so most leaders look for support from those outside the business, typically friends and family. Our leaders showed amazing maturity here, and they also displayed remarkable discretion. They shared their disillusionment only with those closest to them. They turned to people they could, without reservation, trust.

Let's be clear, assuming one's marriage is sound, the strongest and most significant support mechanism during the period of disillusionment is the spouse. Once again, the spouse's focus of support is not to offer advice. In fact, for many of the business or career adversities encountered, the spouse probably has a limited perspective for offering meaningful advice. However, the spouse is someone who will be there, listen, and express genuine concern. At this point of their travails, leaders need support more than they need answers. They need the opportunity to express rather than for someone to "fix" things. Our leaders spoke openly of the "refuge" and "acceptance" they experienced from their spouses.

One leader noted, "I need a good retreat, such as a good family life. This rebuilds self worth . . . and helps me feel good about myself again." Another leader even noted that the spouse (and family) were "the best health club one could have."

Listen to the powerful story of family support that the president of a multinational business shared: "What happens in the business world, when you get the downs, you start having a question or a doubt about your self-worth and your ability to lead and your ability to exercise good decisions and bring value to the organization. Then you go home . . . [and it's] a good family life that all of a sudden brings back that you have been able to instill value. You have been able to bring self worth to the table again. It's that home life that creates that kind of balancing act, so that's what I see. You start feeling good about what you have been able to do when you get home.

"In my position, and I think my management team's position, when things aren't going good at work, the first inclination is not to bring out the whip and draw conclusions about their people. (Instead), they draw conclusions about themselves, their ability to affect change, their ability to bring better operating styles to the table, their ability to affect and implement things properly. That's where the self-doubt comes. That's where the real issue is. So then you go home . . . a good family life and a good home. It has a way of putting everything in perspective."

Here, family provided meaning. The leader recognized that, when all was said and done, the strength and backing of his family would remain. His family provided clear evidence that his life had personal significance outside of the realm of his business.

The importance of the spouse was noted bleakly too. For those whose marriages were troubled or fractious, the lack of support or the inability to turn to the spouse drove a further wedge through the relationship. Some even noted that these events sent clear signals that the marriage could not be saved.

In addition to spouse and family, close friends are important during this stage. Note that these are non-business friends, often people the leaders have known and grown close to over the years. Again, their role is to be there, to listen, and to show concern and consideration.

The support the leaders received was uplifting and encouraging support and not regressive. Others have studied this focus of support, and our outcomes are consistent with those findings. We did not encounter regressive support, in which others acted as enablers, reinforcing and even encouraging the self-pity and depressive decline that can occur during this period.

Recall the leader from the previous chapter who described the pain of being fired. He described coming home on the night of his termination and being met by his wife and children. Then, with remarkable emotion, he notes "By dinner time, my yard was filled with friends, people I've known for years." He went on to say that they didn't talk about the business or how unfairly he'd been treated. "No, they were just there."

These support networks give back to the leaders precisely that which is most deeply threatened during adversity. The support of family and friends lets the leaders know that they are successes, that they are valued and significant, and that people are there in their time of need. As such, personal significance is affirmed and fear is mitigated.

A strong support network can be immeasurably helpful during disillusionment. However, seeking support during a time of need may not be natural for hard driving, "can do" executives. Showing a crack of vulnerability is not what many leaders are about. Not surprisingly, many executives turn away from, not toward, their support networks during these periods.

Further, some leaders may not have cultivated the kind of family relationships or levels of friendships necessary to have an available network of meaningful support. This condition is unfortunate, but understandable. Leaders spend the bulk of their time on business. Any extra time is devoted to family and civic responsibilities (which often have business implications). There simply is little time left for cultivating deep friendships. Acquaintances abound, but friendships may be quite limited. The complexity of this issue is beyond the scope of this book. So, we will simply emphasize, again, the immense value of the support network.

3. Protecting the Image: Behavioral Controls. Most leaders recognize that during this period of disillusionment, the image they project might not be the best for the business. They do not want the message projected by their personal disillusionment sent to the rest of the organization. Leaders are aware of the need to guard and protect the people of the business to the extent possible. Here, they demonstrate the use of behavioral controls.

"I try not to display I'm down. When I'm down, the biggest thing I can do is get out of people's sight." Others noted that they were aware that they were playing a game of impression management during this period. They talked of putting on their game face and psyching themselves into a positive public persona. After all, business must go on. One leader, quite profoundly, commented that "there is fear here, but I can't come across [to the people of the organization] as being fearful."

The contrast between the steady public appearance and the private emotional whirl is worth noting. Reasonably, this contrast represents an additional demand on leaders during a time when the burdens of adversity are already overwhelming. Yet, the logical need for image protection makes sense. Depending on the nature of the adversity, business activities ranging from investor reactions to employee morale could be threatened.

There is no easy answer here. Again, the value of a trusted support network can be a significant help. By allowing the leader to progress quickly through their emotional downtime, the period of public and private contrast can be minimized.

Moving On

Finally, leaders know they need to move through the period of disillusionment quickly. Even while experiencing fear and trauma, successful leaders recognize that they must move forward. They display a strong spirit of resiliency and a clear understanding of the need to rebound.

The leader's overall understanding of the process of disillusionment is very important. As noted earlier, they know that the emotions they are experiencing are natural and reasonable. They do not deny their emotions, but they refuse to be controlled by them.

These leaders are able to act out of necessity and push on. They are not immobilized by disillusionment. They refuse to yield. Let's state it again. Faced with fear and disappointment, these leaders make a decision. They will not allow themselves to languish. They commit to persevere and move ahead.

Return to the managers of the organization mentioned earlier in this chapter who were experiencing the trauma of downsizing and acquisition anxiety. While the emotions at each phase of adversity were similar, the duration and even the intensity of these emotions was not. The managers seemed to move through the disillusionment more quickly with each adversity event.

We believe they were able to do so because they had previously worked through periods of disillusionment. Therefore, they were not afraid of the emotions they experienced. Their adversity memories told them there was something beyond this stage, and it was that hope and expectation that provided the courage to move on. Further, they were able to work through this stage because of their adherence to the logical and healthy process we have described in this chapter.

As you read this, you may want more precise answers. We have described the process of disillusionment, the emotions, and the responses that run through this period. We are often asked how long this period lasts? It depends on the level and intensity of the adversity. Logically, the amount of time depends on the extent to which the categories of adversity are spilling over on one another. But, even for severe and deep cases, successful leaders try to move through this stage quickly. Most of the leaders we interviewed indicated that they try to work through this stage of disillusionment in a couple of days.

Earlier we commented that not everyone who faces the tests of adversity passes with flying colors. Realistically, some fail. These individuals encounter adversity, face disillusionment, and never seem able to move beyond this draining initial stage. They become self-absorbed and wallow in their despair. These people never rebound. They just survive.

Undoubtedly, we have all encountered such people. They have failed to apply the lessons presented in this chapter. Our hope is to provide thoughtful commentary and guidance to help you, as readers, avoid this insidious and destructive trap.

The Wisdom of Experience

Effective leaders experience disillusionment. This is a very emotional phase characterized by a mix and rush of feelings: confusion, uncertainty, despair, and threats to one's very sense of competence. Yet effective leaders seem to know how to accept these feelings as par for the course. It is their first step in exercising some control over an event where their control has been dramatically threatened.

The strategies of control are threefold: cognitive, emotional, and behavioral. Cognitive control consists of placing the event within a larger context of reality. Leaders acknowledge to themselves that this is a temporary event. Like having the flu, they know that health is in their future, but they must accept the feelings of discomfort for the moment.

But they must also exercise emotional controls so that these feelings never gain the upper hand. Either you control the feelings or they will control you. Consequently, our leaders never let the feelings of disillusionment get the upper hand, at least not for long. Yet they never did it alone. They turned to spouses, close friends, and confidants where they could just let their feelings flow, be experienced, and be accepted by people who really cared for them.

Behavioral controls are the third strategy they took to gain control during the phase of disillusionment. They acted as if they were indeed in control. They were not about to panic their followers, but, rather, engaged them in solving a problem by exuding confidence that the problem could be solved.

Another way of labeling these phases is to refer to them as a time for feeling, a time for thought, and a time for action.

11

The Rebound Process: Reflection

"In the face of adversity, we either grow or decline. There is no in-between."

I got real familiar with three o' clock in the morning." The short laugh that followed didn't lessen the intensity of what was being described. The leader's life had been pushed and strained by concurrent struggles from two fronts. Not only was the business going through a difficult period, but also one of his children was fighting a serious illness. He recounted days filled with the stress and emotional weight of trying to keep things going while the pieces just didn't seem to be falling in place.

He would go to bed exhausted, only to awaken between 3:00 and 3:30, his head spinning with ideas and concerns. "I've learned that I can lay there [in bed], but I probably won't go back to sleep anyway. Too many thoughts. My mind is wide-awake. The best thing I can do is just get up and try to sort things out."

Describing these early morning encounters—a unique form of self-confrontation—personal growth seemed to take place. "I did a lot of thinking. I thought about what was happening, what I was doing, and what was really important. I prayed—probably felt closer to God. It was quiet." Then, with philosophic hindsight, he added, "Actually, looking back, those 3 a.m. wake-ups were important time for me. I think they made a big difference as I battled with all that was going on."

Adversity can be a transforming event, prompting leaders to change and grow. Of course, a positive transformation only occurs when leaders have the inner strength to take a tough look at what's going on. Here, leaders must accept adversity and be willing to wrestle with it's impact and consequences.

Often, the leader's ego stands in the way of such confrontation. Recently, best selling business author James Autry was asked how leaders overcome ego. Autry noted that the only way to move beyond ego was to "get into yourself." He went on to comment, "I am always recommending to people that they do something to nurture the inner life, that they try to do something each day that is reflective or meditative . . . In order to get out of the ego, you have to somehow get deeper into your own life."[1]

Reflection—In Search of Meaning

After disillusionment comes reflection, the second phase in the process of bouncing back from adversity. Reflection is a period when leaders immerse themselves in a search for meaning. We found that leaders are searching for answers to four critical questions. Why did this adversity occur? What is the nature of the new situation before me? What does this adversity reveal about me and the business? How must I proceed?

The answers, or attempts to answer, these questions will be unpacked in subsequent chapters. In this chapter, we will begin to explore the all-important process that reveals the answers—the process of reflection.

Although everyone who faces adversity meets some level of disillusionment, the same cannot be said for reflection. Some people do not engage in a logical reflective process. Reflection comes with maturity and requires some degree of emotional security and strength of ego. Reflection, as seen in our opening example, demands self-confrontation and generates self-awareness.

It is impossible to cleanly differentiate the period of disillusionment from the period of reflection. The two generally overlap. In fact, all the leaders interviewed indicated that the process of reflection began immediately. Even while grappling with the uncertainty and despair of disillusionment, these leaders began their search, trying to figure out where they were and what was going on.

Two Approaches

There has been much written about reflection, in both psychological and counseling literature. Our study yielded outcomes that were consistent with much of that work. We found leaders approached reflection from two angles: first, leaders spent time with themselves in introspection; second, they sought input and perspective from others in order to make sense out of the adversity. Although these angles overlap in practice, we will differentiate them so they can be explained more fully and easily.

1. Introspection. Methods of introspection were varied and at times even humorous. Some leaders said they spent a lot of time by themselves in their office. However, most preferred to get away from the regular pattern of business. Their responses ranged from long walks with the family dog to working in the yard. Many, such as our 3 a.m. leader, spoke of waking up early (often unplanned) and using the time for deep personal reflection. Some had cultivated unique ways to get away and just think through what was happening. One leader noted, "I go home and get on the tractor and mow the yard. My wife will come out and say 'The kids cut that grass yesterday.' I'll just say that I know and keep going."

Introspection is clearly a time of soul searching. Remember, as we have discussed earlier, leaders are trying to find answers to their questions about their personal significance and sense of control. Additionally, although they may have difficulty naming the emotion, they are often battling a fear of failure.

We are not overstating the case to say that leaders question their very essence. One of the leaders we talked with, fresh on the heels of a significant crisis, described this period as a time of deep soul-searching. The leader noted that crises create a "forced introspection for those who generally have no time for introspection."

What do leaders do during this phase of introspection? First, they think through the information and evidence they have and the situation that now exists because of the adversity. They run through it over and over again. They look for patterns. They look for things they may have missed.

The following example may help clarify this process of introspection. We interviewed the president of a service business who, over a lengthy two-year period, had endured a string of business adversities: an entrepreneurial venture failed to meet expectations, a key executive had to be dismissed, the core market became increasingly competitive and cutthroat in nature. He noted that he could feel his energy and personal resilience being drained. He described periods of introspection occurring in the early morning hours of the day. These early morning "personal retreats" became part of his routine. He soon recognized that this was a great time to think and put things in perspective. He further noted that this reflective time helped provide the frame of mind he needed to get through what he knew would be the exhausting demands of the coming day.

Since introspection involves a fundamental search for personal significance, it was not surprising that many spoke of a spiritual dimension to their introspection. These leaders indicated that their personal religious faith and their spiritual connection played a key role in their introspective search. For these leaders, turning to their faith in the midst of confusion and loss provided three outcomes. First, their faith and spirituality provided a calming base of assurance that adversity could be met and addressed. Second, faith provided a different lens for viewing the presence, causes, and ramifications of adversity. Third, for those whose reflections included prayer, new insights and perspective were gained.

Importantly, all of the leaders spoke of the introspective period as an important developmental point. Introspection grounded them and even led to humility. One of our leaders explained this grounding and humility in context. He noted that in the pace of business activity, leaders can easily get caught up in their own self-importance. Of course, as the business succeeds and performs better and better, this realm of self-importance can grow. Adversity and introspection humbles leaders. It is a healthy brush with reality. "Humility is always a powerful developmental ally because it allows us to become open to new options and alternatives."

2.Time with Others. In addition to introspection, reflection also includes the need to reach out to others. We saw a different support network in this period than during disillusionment. Family and friends were less important. Instead, trusted business colleagues and recognized experts were sought out. Generally, these were people outside of the leader's business, but they were people with experiences and backgrounds that enabled them to shed light on what was going on. Typically, they were business and organizational leaders themselves.

These peers and experts offered ideas, options, and possibilities. They shared similar situations and discussed the approaches they tried. They knew both failure and success. Their input was so valuable because they could relate, provide insight and perspective, and come up with solutions.

Many of these were informal associations between business friends and associates. Typically, these associations started as leaders met to work together on a common task, a community project, for example. As the years passed, they would get together every so often for lunch, and build a closer bond. Openness and trust was built over time. When problems arose, each would bounce ideas off the other. These relationships endured because of their reciprocal nature.

In some cases, the leader contacts were more formally structured, usually through leader networks like the Young Presidents Organization (YPO). In these network organizations, leaders could offer options and help one another recognize the nature and context of what was going on. For example, one leader talked of sharing a particularly demoralizing business crisis with a small support cadre from YPO. As he explained the business crisis and personal trauma of shifting a business unit and laying off people he cared about, he became aware that his colleagues' heads were nodding as the story unfolded. Finally, one of them smiled calmly and supportively said, "Welcome to the club. We've all been through the same thing."

One of the literary giants of the early 20th century, Edward Morgan Forster, was fond of saying: "I don't know what I think until I can see what I say." Conversation with trusted colleagues provides an opportunity to test out ideas, clarify thoughts, and develop and try out various plans of action. It is an indispensable part of the rebound process.

Putting It All Together

It's probably evident that the reflective period coincides with the typical operating style of most leaders. They are searching for information. Information comes from personal introspection, careful discussions with others, and study and analysis. Leaders are digging to find out as much as they can in an effort to make sense out of what is going on. Successful leaders want to be informed and this is a process of seeking that information and pondering what it really means.

A Spark of Creativity

The period of reflection is transforming because it opens avenues for creativity. In other words, the very nature of reflection fosters new approaches and new ways of thinking. Let's explain that more fully.

Considerable research has looked at how creativity can be encouraged in today's organizations.[2] This research suggests that creativity often emerges when a unique and somewhat nontraditional decision-making approach is used.[3] The keys to this approach lie in the processes of immersion and incubation.

Immersion occurs when one takes the time to study a problem or issue in depth. We plunge into the issue, explore it carefully, ask tough questions, and look at it from all angles. All possibilities and all conceivable explanations are considered. The goal during immersion is to defer judgment and conclusion until we consider a range of ideas. We are searching for new views and new connections. This process of becoming immersed in the adversity issues is exactly what leaders do during reflection.

Immersion is followed by incubation. In simplest terms, incubation comes when we take time to step back from all the thoughts, ideas, and insights that have been generated. We take some time just to mull over all the input we have gathered.

Incubation involves a period of rumination and subconscious processing. Connections and links are drawn together. Something happens as we struggle, seek new perspectives, and think through what is occurring. The outcome is often a creative angle or a novel approach.

Consider the following example. Roger Kelley is an amazing leader whose approach to life and the challenges of leadership has shaped the careers of many executives. Through his long career, Roger has been a top-ranking executive, a governmental leader, and an entrepreneur. You may not recognize his name, but undoubtedly he has touched you and your family. In the early 1970s, with our country embroiled in the Vietnam conflict, Roger was asked to take a leave of absence from his business career. He was asked to move to Washington to serve as an Assistant Secretary of Defense. His charge was to revamp the system of military draft that was in place at the time. Roger, along with others, was convinced the current draft system, with its extended process of deferments, was unfair and biased against those of lower socio-economic status.

The problem was clear, pervasive, and escalating daily. But what was the answer? Realizing that the answer was not to be found at the Pentagon, Roger went to work. For six months, he met with people at all levels of the military. He dove in submarines, flew in jets, and visited aircraft carriers. He met with officers and enlisted men alike. He asked for ideas. He recorded his findings and carefully pondered them. Eventually, the answer came—an all-volunteer army. The concept evolved, step-by-step, through an intense period of study.[4]

Our guess is that many of you have probably experienced something similar to this pattern. You have struggled with an adversity, perhaps a significant business problem. You have spent time in introspection and consulted with trusted colleagues. The adversity and the need for a strategy of action pressed on your mind even as the ongoing, day-to-day activities of business life were handled. Over time, ideas came together, and a new path seemed clear.

The ideas that come from reflection are often portrayed as blinding flashes of insights. These epiphanies, these classic "ah-ha" experiences, are exciting to hear, and they make dramatic stories. But, it's rarely the way successful leaders gain insight. Instead, the real insight, the new idea, the new path, usually comes gradually from hard work and dedicated reflection.

A Commitment to Reflection

Leaders are driven to reflection by adversity. However, a number of leaders realized that the reflective time was so powerful, so shaping and developmental, that they committed to building it into their regular regimen of executive activity. Often this was done through formal support mechanisms. YPO has already been noted, and over a third of our group had YPO ties. Others had standing meetings on their schedules with other leaders. These groups were usually quite small and rarely exceeded a handful of people. Again, such groups functioned and survived because of the give-and-take nature of their interactions.

The length of the period of reflection varies. It changes, as one would surmise, based on the nature of the adversity.

However, most of the leaders we interviewed described reflection lasting from a few days to a few weeks. But there were exceptions, as seen in the Roger Kelley story.

As noted above, some leaders find the reflection process that they encounter during adversity to reveal deep personal meaning. They take steps to incorporate reflective time into their regular schedules.

The Wisdom of Experience

The unreflective life is not a human life. It's a life of instinct that only gets you through the day. Reflection is a time of searching. Often, it includes deep soul searching. Questions about one's own competency are at stake as are solutions to real problems.

It's a tricky time. The leader needs to depersonalize the event in order to deal with it as objectively as possible. On the other hand, it is an opportunity for leaders to learn something about themselves, to see themselves as others see them. Of course, leaders can easily slip into defending a bruised ego and blind themselves to any personal learning and, most likely, any creative solutions to the problems that lie before them.

Reflection allows for the opportunity to examine one's worldview, basic values, duties, and responsibilities, as well as significant life goals. As a result, a larger context is created within which the leader can examine and evaluate the disruptive event of adversity to be confronted. Reflection creates the conditions necessary for the appearance of a solution and a path to a crisis resolution.

The act of reflection always involves drawing upon the leader's basic beliefs, values, experiences, and faith as a way of evaluating and formulating an action plan. But this does not occur in a vacuum. Leaders also need to talk about their reflection with trusted friends and associates. In this way, they test out their insights and the consequences of various courses of intended action.

THE PATH
THROUGH ADVERSITY–
TRANSFORMATION

12

The Rebound Transformation Process: Defining Your Foundation

"The tougher things are, the more focused you have to be."

Early in our conversations, we asked the leaders to describe the event or experience that had been the most critical in shaping their careers. Often, these defining events dealt with adversities and lessons learned through the struggle of adversity. A number of these experiences involved tragedies or near tragedies that had invaded the leaders' lives. In that light, the following story stands as a riveting example of the leader rebound.

A successful entrepreneur, business owner, and community leader, she recounted the event with clarity in spite of the 17 years that had since elapsed. She told of her hectic work schedule, extensive traveling, and a bitterly cold day in late December. "I got up in the morning and went to the basement. The house was very cold . . . We were having a severe winter. It was 25 degrees below zero. . . The house had an old, round-belly coal furnace that had been converted into a gas furnace. I went down to light that furnace, and I reached in with my right hand with a Bic lighter. Just as I was ready to turn on the lighter to light the pilot, I heard a bird. It caused me to look over my left shoulder at the same time that the furnace blew up." She recalled the hospital and the severe burns on her face, arms, and chest. It was a unique and unforgettable experience.

She spoke with the greatest intensity about the burn bath, part of her medical treatment. "When they bathe you, you have raw skin because it has to be opened. It's exceedingly painful. They gave me my first burn bath, and I said, 'that is the last burn bath you ever give me. From now on I will do my own.'" She noted that her doctor, no doubt wishing to encourage her fighting spirit, allowed her dictate to be followed. "I did my own bandaging in the hospital and was out of there in 11 days. That experience has had a real lasting impact on me for my whole life. It was like, OK, let's get going. I may not know what I'm going to do, but I really just want to do whatever I can do every day and go for it. . . Everything happens for a reason."

The trauma of her adversity event prompted movement. She returned to her business with a new direction and zeal. She committed to a new business focus, involving ventures she had pondered but hadn't been able to act on due to the risks involved. This leader displayed a persevering attitude, and she is a wonderful example of the spirit of rebound. She allowed herself to be transformed by the crisis she faced. She emerged from her personal crisis with an energized outlook toward business and life.

Reflection and Revelation

The result of the personal reflection process was usually some new awareness or insight. At times, our leaders gained insight or revelation about business and the nature of relationships. Often, however, they gained insight about their own character. In short, the leaders' very foundations were being revealed. It is this latter theme that we will address in this chapter.

The period of reflection often moves leaders to a deeper level of understanding where they define or redefine themselves. Indeed, many leaders, like the woman in our opening example, view adversity as a defining experience. Adversity forces them to take a hard, reflective look at themselves. Through this experience, leaders learn what they truly believe, and how they intend to respond. This level, where they define their personal foundations, can be life changing.

When confronted with deep adversities or crises, the route out always begins by finding your personal foundations. One leader called this encounter the "starting point" in trying to figure out "what really matters." Another referred to such encounters as "golden moments." In short, reflection gave leaders an eye-opening view of themselves, revealing their personal foundations, values, and character. This became the bedrock of the rebound transformation.

Leaders express and reveal their foundations, values, and character every day through the things that they say and do, as well as the things they do not say and do not do. In our era, the media questions leader character and values. Consequently, the themes of values and character take on added importance.

Values and character are often elusive concepts. Yet, under the press of adversity, leaders are forced to take a tough look at these themes. One leader called it "gut check time." It can be humbling. It can also be a time of grounding when leaders ask themselves who they are and what they are about. They often reconsider core personal values and rethink the basics. As author Delores Ambrose aptly noted, in order to transform organizations, leaders must first transform themselves.[1]

Four Personal Areas

When leaders check their foundations, they are forced to explore four personal arenas. Each offers an important theme for the leader.

The Four Corners of Personal Foundation

- *Rediscovering Significance and What Really Counts*

- *Reaffirming Core Values*

- *Accepting Limits*

- *Recognizing What You Can't Control*

1. Rediscovering Significance: What Really Counts? Ken Melrose is the chairman and CEO of the Toro Company. He assumed the presidency only to be greeted by a worldwide economic recession and the company's first operating loss in over 35 years. In his own words, "Everything seemed to be going wrong."[2] The recovery and subsequent success of Toro is a story of insightful strategic thinking, careful implementation, and persistence.

Melrose tells a wonderful story of being trained to become a lay teacher for his church. At one of the training sessions, a guest speaker, a rabbi, addressed the trainees and encouraged them to consider the purpose of life. The rabbi pressed and prodded the group, urging them to look at their work and to consider their legacy. He pointed out that their children and perhaps even their grandchildren might remember them and a few of their accomplishments. However, with almost absolute certainty, their great-great-grandchildren would have no idea who they were or what they had done.

Melrose found this realization both powerful and sobering. "What is the purpose of life? If I'll mean nothing at all to those just four generations ahead, why am I here?"[3]

Melrose was asking the fundamental questions. They are the questions that surface during adversity, particularly deep adversity and crisis. Why am I here? What is my purpose? What really counts? Rarely do leaders take the time to step back and embrace these tough questions during their normal cycle of business activity. But crises force them to do so.

One of the most creative and charismatic leaders we interviewed boasted an impressive 20-year history of business success. Rapid expansion and double-digit growth marked most years. Against this positive backdrop, the last two years stood in stark contrast. They were years of high profile setbacks. Two major projects had gone bad, each gaining considerable public exposure. A personal health crisis had required extensive hospitalization. A restructuring of the leadership team had taken place. We didn't know what to expect as we began our interview to explore dimensions of success. We were greeted with a remarkable, even surprising, display of commitment and resilience.

Reflecting on this period, the CEO commented on a personal search for meaning. "There's been so many ups and downs . . . Both personally and career wise, there hasn't been the steadiness. It's been really up or really down. I think the inner strength makes a big difference . . . but I've had some really tough times…"

As the CEO talked about the reflection and soul-searching of this time, a profound perspective was offered. "I think it affected my career in a positive way in that it made me very introspective during those times… You see [people] taking advantage of a situation… just to get that last dollar... not contributing to a cause as they should have...How many hearses have you seen that have a U-Haul behind them?...It made me realize, you know, you're not going to have until you're 50, 60, 70 years old to correct and move on..." This CEO was dealing with the key question, "what really counts?"

All the leaders found the same answer. We have talked about it and defined it earlier in the book, and its reappearance will come as no surprise. At their core and at this point of grounding, leaders want significance. They want the sense that what they do really counts, really matters, and really has an impact.

Successful leaders transfer this notion of "what really counts" into a personal mission. The personal mission is the leader's conception of what they will do and what they will contribute. The leader's personal mission is as close as they can come to defining their focus of significance.

Make no mistake, the leader's quest is for significance. It provides meaning and perspective to the life work of the leader. It is, as we have carefully framed, the benchmark against which the leader's personal sense of success is measured. A leader's encounter with adversity often forces him or her to ask whether the current path leads toward significance and therefore success.

Kim Polese is co-founder, chairman and chief strategy officer of Marimba. A star in the high tech industry, Polese cut her corporate teeth at Sun Microsystems as part of the core team that developed Java. She has faced plenty of challenges at Marimba. In 2000, her COO left the rapidly expanding company just as the tech market went into its turbulent and uncertain downspin. Polese, understandably, spread herself too thin. She stepped back, took steps to strengthen the management team and committed to taking a long-term approach to the business that she believed would build real success. She summed up her driving philosophy in the succinct terms we've heard before, "I want to leave a legacy, something that matters and benefits people."[4]

Many leaders struggle at this point. Why am I working these ungodly hours? Why am I making these sacrifices? Is this what I should be doing? Would I feel happier and more content elsewhere? These questions move many leaders to make changes in their careers. In some cases, change involves moving to a different organization, presumably where the challenges more closely match the leader's sense of personal mission.

Recall our example of Dee from an earlier chapter. She was the fast-tracker who was passed over for the vice presidency she so dearly desired. After extended soul searching and a couple of frank discussions with her boss, she realized that she would not find the significance she needed with her current employer. She made a life-changing decision to leave the business. Today, she is with a smaller firm. While second-in-command, her working relationship with her new boss is collaborative. Dee and her employer form a leadership team. Dee is finally gaining the challenge and sense of achievement that she has craved for some time.

Like Dee, some leaders changed their career paths entirely. "It was something I was looking for. I was looking on, really focused on something I wanted to do and where I could do it. So I was looking…Management skills transfer. They just flat out transfer."

Some noted that the "what really counts" inquiry pushed them to approach their business differently. One leader summarized succinctly, "You begin to question who you are and what you do. [This] may lead to a reallocation of time and effort." Refocusing time, effort, and energy was a common theme, and it yielded a variety of directions. Comments ranged from making sure everybody understood the direction of the business to spending more time rallying support and making sure people were "on board."

The depth and importance of this reflective step cannot be emphasized too strongly. To push to the foundations, to ask what really counts, can be painful and exacting. Yet, for those leaders who go the distance and allow themselves to probe at this personal level, revelation comes and they are transformed by the insights gained.

2. Reaffirming Core Values. Adversity forces leaders to get in touch with their core personal values. Core personal values are those beliefs and themes that are so critical and fundamental that they cannot be mitigated or compromised. The direction out of deep adversity and crisis begins with an understanding of what really counts, and the path traveled must be defined by core values.

One CEO offered a penetrating story. He spoke of growing competition in his industry. The competitive demands pushed one particular competitor to cut corners and shade specifications in order to present bids that would win business. The leader's firm lost a lot important business, and most of it had gone to this competitor. Eventually, as the losses mounted, the leader's organization faced a pending crisis. The CEO and his executive team struggled to find the route out. The business decline had to be reversed. Jobs were at stake.

The company took the high ground. They maintained their integrity. They refused to play deceptive games and continued to stress their quality and dependability, even at the higher cost. The executive commented, "I wasn't sure if this was the best bottom-line decision, but I knew it was the only one we could live with." Over time, the tactics of the competition came to light, and the CEO's firm regained and expanded market share as major customers abandoned the competitor.

We always concluded our leader interviews with the same question: What words of wisdom and words of advice would you offer to young emerging leaders as they begin their leadership journey? "Have a real good understanding of yourself," was the most common insight they offered. "Know and feel a purpose in life." "Know what you stand for or you'll fall for anything." "Have an acute recognition of who you are, what you value, and how you intend to contribute."

Our leaders revealed a consistent list of core personal values. These were seen as guiding principles that became particularly relevant during adversity. These core values included integrity, honesty, respect, fair dealings, and persistence. One leader even went so far as to say that when one begins to break from these values, "it's the path to failure."

Another leader put this in perspective, noting that in the depth of adversity, there is a point where "you never really know what to do. You just keep doing things until you find the key. You stick to the principles and just keep going."

3. Identifying and Accepting Limits. Understanding your limits is another part of finding your foundation. It entails recognizing your shortcomings, but goes even further. Recognizing limits is where the leader realizes and admits what he or she cannot and will not be.

Certainly, adversity harshly introduces those limits. We all know no one person has all the answers, and no one is omnipotent. But it's quite a different thing to see evidence of our glitches and imperfections. "I guess I don't spend enough time on the people stuff." "I was looking down the road and maybe didn't keep focused enough on the day-to-day operations." These insights were truly reality checks.

Successful leaders are short on excuses here and long on accepting these insights for their basic truth and value. This is an important distinction. Typically, there are numerous reasons for the shortcomings. Some deal with personal preferences: "I'm more comfortable with the technical, analytic approach to things." Many deal with the cold realization that there is not enough time to take care of everything. But leaders refuse to dodge their shortcomings by presenting excuses. In fact, they probe to see what the knowledge of these shortcomings actually means.

One of our leaders commented that his struggle with adversity finally brought him face to face with the realization that he was pursuing a course of business that just wasn't right for him. Ventures went beyond what the business knew and beyond what he was comfortable handling.

One CEO offered a touching perspective on this theme. The CEO recounted, with great flair and pride, the entrepreneurial talents that had built a very successful business. He had his fingers in all phases of the business. Not surprisingly, his people knew this and consistently stepped back and deferred to the CEO's judgment. Commenting on his free-wheeling entrepreneurial style, he quipped about how he handled problems, "You know, I'll walk in a meeting and say, well if that person's not fitting, move them or move them on." But he failed to take the broad strokes needed to put a cadre of talented leaders in place. Facing a significant personal health crisis, he realized that some staff moves had to occur. Recognizing that he could not handle everything himself, he brought in needed talent. "That brought a level of increased professionalism and structure here, which led to growth. It [the health crisis] forced an issue that I think wouldn't have happened for another two to three years, and I think the company would have had some big problems."

As in the case above, many leaders felt their limits would not have been tested without the presence of adversity or crisis. These tests forced them to admit and address limitations, which allowed future progress and improvement.

4. Rethinking Control and Recognizing What Can't Be Controlled. Control is another element that must be addressed while exploring personal foundations. As leaders begin to understand their limits, they begin to see what they cannot control. Rather than being a depressing insight, our leaders suggested that this insight, once recognized and accepted, has a liberating quality. It gave them the opportunity to turn loose everything beyond their realm of influence.

To tell people not to worry about things over which they have no control is good advice. However, that advice is based on the assumption that people know what they are unable to control. Adversity provides the lesson. Adversity identifies the leader's inability to control all things.

By realizing that some events are simply beyond their capacity to ever control, leaders are able to relieve themselves of the punishing burden of believing they can do what they know in their hearts they cannot. Often, this means putting their faith in something beyond themselves. And therein comes the liberating impact.

Consider the words and example of one of our leaders. "I think as I have matured and my horizon and my experiences have matured, I just don't sweat things. I'm not saying I'm not concerned, and I don't do things to remedy the situation. But I don't sit there and sweat and worry about things like I used to." He went on to say he prepared and covered the bases as best he could. Yet, he had learned that worrying about what could not be controlled was folly.

The Wisdom of Experience

Adversity drives leaders back to their personal foundations. In fact, the way out of adversity starts with an individual's answer to basic questions such as the purpose of life and what matters most. These questions, stimulated by the crisis, force leaders to review their fundamental beliefs, which serve as anchors in a sea of uncertainty.

Ultimately, leaders want to make a difference and do something that really matters. This is the source of their personal mission, and their passion is to achieve that mission. From this perspective, no crisis can stop them; they have an obligation to pursue their mission. Since this is a personal mission, the odds of success do not matter.

Adversity also forces them to review and call upon their core values. And it is these core values that guide them in their decisions and throughout the rebound process. No matter what course of action they decide upon, it has to be conducted with integrity, honesty, respect, fair dealings, and with perseverance. In the end, leaders talk about having to be true to themselves and their values. There is only going to be one face in the mirror when they look, and they want it to be an honorable one.

The revelations of adversity make leaders aware of their limits as well as their destiny. To be aware of what one can and cannot be, do and not do, accept or not accept, and control or not control is liberating. Accordingly, leaders are better able to focus their energies and attention on what really matters.

13

The Rebound Transformation Process: Defining the Adversity Situation

"You can't fix it until you understand it."

He was a seasoned executive with nearly 30 years of corporate leadership experience. Confident and self-assured, his business success was nearly matched by his high-profile presence in the community. But he didn't hesitate, and he didn't pull any punches when asked about adversity. He went back, and like so many others, recalled one key adversity event with amazing clarity. His business faced bankruptcy: "I was embarrassed… It was a shock to the ego." He went on. "I had to focus. Pull control back. What will it take to get control back?"

"One way to get control back is to understand you can't control everything. Ask what [are] the most important things . . . You can't fix it until you understand it. You can't fix it until you understand all the issues and problems… I have to know the situation even if I don't know how to fix it…Even if I don't know every step along the way… If I can redefine the situation—redefine to put me back in control…Once I understand the situation, I know what steps to take."

In this chapter, we talk about the necessity of coming to grips with the situation that adversity presents. Often, for the leader, this means defining or redefining the situation. Why is there a need for redefinition? Perhaps, GE's Jack Welch said it best when he

described the principles ingrained in his company, "See reality—see the world the way it is, not the way you wish it to be."[1]
Adversity forces leaders to address a new world. It is a harsh wake-up call signaling the situation has changed. Therefore, successful leaders must think through, grasp, and accurately define the real situation.

A Brush with Reality

Redefining the situation is the second step in transformation. It involves an adjustment, usually an adjustment in thinking and perspective. It requires an honest look at what is really happening. In many cases, adversity prompts a brush with reality.

Leaders often live in a protected world. Messages are screened. Input is filtered. Many people offer the leader only favorable information. Of course, leaders can be deluded through this process. They can believe their own press. Therefore, what is revealed through adversity may be a cold, tough dose of reality. Adversity shakes the leader and says, "This is what is really going on."

The leader may gain insight about how the business is approached and operated. Practices and policies already in place may need to be reconsidered or changed. Or, the reality may extend beyond the business. Some of our leaders discovered the reality of family or personal problems. Despite signals that family relations were fraying, that marital relations were strained, or even that personal health was endangered, these themes became real only after being brought into the leader's radar scan. Generally, this eye-opening look was revealed through adversity.

While leaders know that adversities will come, adversity experiences often do not make sense. They are confusing and distracting. Since adversity is not the expected or anticipated outcome, it does not fit cleanly into leaders' plans. They ask, "Why this? Why now?" The loss of control that the leaders speak of so passionately is due, in a large measure, to the confusion over what is actually taking place. The leaders need to make sense out of events by defining or redefining the situation.

The interviewed leaders were clear. While they engaged in deep introspection, searched their souls, and gained new insights and revelations, they were seeking to make sense of adversity and crisis. While rather seamless in practice, the reflection and definition stages do differ. Largely, the questioning and searching of reflection takes place with the hope that an understanding and redefinition of the adversity will become apparent. Accordingly, leaders looked for logic and meaning. Even when the exact path out of a crisis was obscured, they felt a powerful need to be able to define what was happening. As the leader in the opening vignette said, once he understood the situation, he could begin to act, even if he didn't know every step along the way.

Of course, redefinition comes through asking questions and soul-searching. The leader might ask, "Why did it happen? Who has the answers? How did I get in this state? What do I do now?" By asking these questions leaders may not gain the full picture, but they emerge with a refined sense of what has happened and where they stand. One of our leaders, with emotion and profundity, noted, "Adversities are not overcome but understood."

The Need for Definition

We learned that every adversity needs to be defined. To define a personal health problem, leaders talk to the best doctors, read the latest reports, engage in deep personal reflection, and finally come to the point where they are able to say, "OK, so this is what I'm up against." While unsure of the road ahead, knowing the lay of the land enables leaders to develop a plan and a response.

Understanding the problem gives leaders a sense of control, but their definition of control at this stage is quite interesting. When the interviewed leaders spoke of control, they did not mean the ability to manipulate and orchestrate everything that went on. While that may have been desirable, they knew it was impossible. To them, a sense of control comes from understanding the foundations and events. This lets them consider options and develop a method of response.

We saw the same thing in business crises. Most noted that the exact strategy was less important, at least initially, than getting a firm grasp on what they faced.

Consider the following example: When Buck Buchanan, former NFL Hall-of-Fame lineman and founder of All Pro Construction in Kansas City, died of lung cancer, his widow, Virginia, faced both a personal and business crises. However, contrary to the advice of nearly everyone, Virginia refused to sell the business and instead, she assumed the presidency. She was at ground zero, knowing practically nothing of the business. She admitted being terrified at the prospect of taking over. She had little experience and was a woman in a male-dominated industry. Further, she was a black woman in a field where few blacks held leadership positions.

The first thing she did was to gain a clear understanding of where the business actually stood. The picture was bleak indeed. She had no idea how bad things had gotten during Buck's long illness. Cash flow problems, employee dissension, underestimated bids that produced losing contracts, and the list went on and on. Yet this understanding and definition of the situation were critical precursors to any subsequent plan.[2]

The Defining Process

In clearest terms, at this juncture the leaders were trying to figure out exactly what they faced as a result of their adversity experience. To understand their hurdle, they relied on personal insights, careful study and reflection, and the advice and counsel of others.

Leaders go through a fairly consistent process in attempting to define the situation and thereby establish a plan of action. In almost every case they follow a logical sequence. Let's look at the elements of this sequence.

1. Relying on Personal Experiences. Most leaders initially turn to their personal experiences to understand and grasp the situation. Here, leaders ask, "Is this situation similar to other experiences I have had?" One leader expressed a common theme. When he looked carefully at the dynamics of adversity, he recognized that he had previous experience to draw upon. "I know the cure because I've been there before."

This base of personal experiences seems to be reasonable for a number of reasons. First, it is quick and direct. Second, it does not drag others into the adversity, allowing the leader to avoid the embarrassment that might come from sharing everything that's going on or has gone wrong. Third, as noted above, leaders often do have experiences that allow them to define the new situation clearly and accurately.

However, a major caveat must be raised. If the adversity has arisen because of the leader's mistakes or misreadings of the current situation, relying on personal experience may not provide the breadth of background necessary to fully define the situation and all the dimensions it contains. Most of the leaders we talked with recognized this caution. In fact, they had a tendency to not turn to personal experiences as their starting point. Instead, they tended to gather as much information as they could as a first step. Then personal experiences became part of the sifting and defining process. They seemed to be aware that if they turned to personal experience first, they could fall into the trap of seeking out and selectively screening information that would merely validate their experiences and biases. Therefore, contrary to natural inclinations, personal experiences are not a solid starting point.

2. Gaining Outside Information. Successful leaders actively searched for information and frequently turned to outside sources to help them understand the dynamics of the adversity situation. Listen to the words of one leader, "I come to grips with realities. I look outside our organization to find out what's going on—to gather insight on what's happening. I need information, and I realize we are not the only ones to miss something."

Faced with the need to gain information, leaders talk to those in their leader networks. They also turn to recognized experts in the field. Additionally, they spend time studying the situation, and poring through reports and projections. All the while, they are trying to bridge connections between these outside sources and their personal experiences.

3. Interpersonal Reflection and Analysis. Armed with information, leaders are ready for a period of interpersonal reflection and analysis. Note the distinction, personal introspection and reflection have already been taking place. Now, leaders are ready to draw others into the situation and use collective insight to be sure the situation is fully understood. The key internal players come together to share issues and information and to attain a collective grasp of the situation.

While we have been describing efforts to understand the lay of the situation for business-related adversity, the pattern is the same for other types of adversities. We saw the same pattern when family adversities were present and when personal health crises were present. For example, one leader described coming to grips with a life-threatening health issue and recognizing its business impact. First, the best medical experts were consulted. Then, the leader figured out what made the most sense. Finally, the top staff was called together for an open discussion to make sure all dimensions of the adversity were understood.

Andy Grove, CEO of Intel, described this very process in *Fortune* magazine. He discovered, "oh, my God," that he had prostate cancer.[3] After his initial shock of how a healthy and physically active person like him could have prostate cancer, he set out to discover all he could about this disease. His research revealed a lot of uncertainty and debate among the medical profession about which course of treatment was best. In fact, he said, "the field was hopping, not just with new work and discoveries, but with controversy." Every medical specialty favored its own approach. What should the non-medical specialist and patient do?

To gather data, he read articles and made appointments with specialists. He looked at the findings for various procedures. He even found a procedure that he referred to as "smart bomb" radiation, with high effectiveness and minimal side effects. This procedure was called high-dose-rate radiation. A variant of the seed technique, it left no permanent seeds in the prostate.

Of course, in the end, he had to make a decision based on an analysis of the best probabilities, without any absolute certainty. By sharing his journey publicly, he has raised the level of awareness among men and their loved-ones. This awareness is not just about prostate cancer and various treatments. Grove also fostered awareness and a demonstration of the necessity for each individual to take charge of his own disease.

The Outcomes of Definition

Leaders undertake the defining process to yield outcomes and provide answers. In general, they seek three outcomes. First, leaders try to figure out the key issues at stake. Adversity often forces leaders to look carefully at the issues and in some cases to redefine the issues. Leaders are careful at this point. They want to move with some speed, but also be certain that they have identified the proper issues. In defining the real issues, past experiences often resurface. One leader described it this way, "Different situation, different cast of characters, same issues."

Second, leaders want to identify why they are in the situation? Answering this question reveals a great deal about a leader's character and ability to rebound. In some cases, leaders identify a reason for the adversity: "We lost sight of our focus." "In order to get the people we needed, we probably didn't pay enough attention to them." "We got caught up [in one phase of the business] and let others slip." Logically, if one can put together such an explanation, the route out becomes clearer.

However, the explanation of why the situation exists is not always clear. In fact, given the fickle nature of adversity, often our leaders had a rather incomplete or imprecise reason why they were in the situation. Sometimes, the economy shifts, the body wears down, or a major customer suddenly changes expectations and demands. The reasons are fuzzy at best.

Successful leaders do the best they can. They understand the value in defining the causes. At the same time, they seem to accept that some adversity foundations will remain nebulous. Accordingly, they attempt to move to a third outcome with reasonable speed and diligence.

Here, leaders seek to define the immediate point of corrective action. While this may seem to be a straightforward issue, there is considerable depth to this point. Leaders are determining the specific problems that must be solved immediately. While they understand the importance of a broad or comprehensive strategic approach, they recognize that certain immediate issues must be addressed in order to move beyond adversity and progress. This is especially true during crisis when survival is threatened. There are actions that must be made now, today.

Importantly, leaders realize that the definition of the situation will shift as they address the adversity. Some of the corrective steps may work, but be too limited. Some of the corrective steps may reveal deeper issues that require attention. Sometimes as events unfold, we realize that our initial points of corrective action were ill-placed or ineffective. Therefore, this form of situational analysis has to be a continuing activity.

The Wisdom of Experience

Adversity is an occasion to see the world with clearer eyes and make sense out of crisis. The only way to do that is to try to see the world as objectively and dispassionately as possible. Adversity can be a wake-up call, challenging your perceptions of reality and forcing you to see the world as it really is. Yet this is the only way that effective plans of corrective action can be formulated.

The first step in acquiring some control or command over adversity is to achieve a good understanding or definition of the situation. Knowing what you are up against is not always as easy as it seems. But it's a fundamental step that can bring even more adversity if missed.

Getting a firm grasp on reality requires more than drawing upon your own set of experiences. It demands getting outside yourself and all the emotions that color your view of the world. Consequently, accurate information and feedback must be sought from employees, customers, experts, and friends. With accurate information our leaders were able to prioritize the key issues and draw upon their own experiences in evaluating the situation.

But more than information is needed. Wise decisions require reflection and reflective dialogue with others to determine the best course of action. And this was characteristic of all the leaders we interviewed.

Of course, similar to most business activities, leaders are forced to make decisions without ever having all the information they want or need. They have to set off in a direction without any guarantees that they are not heading down a dead end.

14

Reframing Adversity into Challenge

"I took it as a challenge."

He spoke precisely, carefully, as he told the story. It was a story of resurrecting a business against trying odds. The story had added meaning and depth as he recounted his leadership role.

"It was all consuming…We were headed down the tube. So, for several years, I was committed, as much as anybody has ever been committed to the company and to a job—to a mission. It was more than a job. It was more of the company's mission to save [the business]. And, without being too melodramatic, there didn't seem to be too many other folks that took an interest…But I took it as a challenge because I knew there were thousands…that depended on [the business]…So yeah, I got a lot of feelings of success when the place survived that period. And I still feed off that just a little bit."

As the conversation continued, we noticed something interesting. As he recalled the depths of this trying time, he did not use the terms crisis or adversity. Instead, he spoke of challenge.

We have unfolded the adversity process carefully and methodically because we don't want to oversimplify everything that is going on. Generally, we only see successful leaders with the capacity to approach adversity as a challenge and move through it with courage. All the foundational pieces—the struggle, disillusionment, introspective soul searching, grounding, and situational perspective—aren't apparent to an outsider. All we see is a bold, resilient leader, somehow turning an overwhelming adversity into a personal challenge. The leader appears as a superhero of sorts, responding in ways that seem amazing and surreal.

We hope, by now, you see that there is more. Leaders are talented but they are not superhuman. They have learned how to approach adversity. It is a systematic method, grounded in a solid understanding of the role of adversity in life. Their approach is basic and psychologically healthy, but it's nothing more than that.

We have been careful to emphasize this truth because it underscores the assurance that the leader's rebound is available to each of us, regardless of our level of leadership. Further, while this is a lesson of leadership, it is, importantly, a lesson of life.

Reframing

The idea of a reframe is drawn from psychology and counseling literature. Simply stated, reframe means looking at situations and events differently. We all have the ability to reframe, and we use this capacity regularly.

Reframing occurs when we view events through new lenses. Accordingly, our view is affected by a slightly different, comparative view, which leads us to rethink what we see or feel. Of course, there is nothing novel here. We've all had the reframe experience.

When your boss informs you that your salary increase for next year will only be a 2 percent bump over the current year, you feel disappointed and frustrated. You worked hard. You performed. In fact, by any objective criteria, you were one of the unit's top performers. A 2 percent raise for all that work is unfair, and your satisfaction and motivation teeter at the brink of decline.

Add one more piece of information. You learn that due to severe cutbacks, all raises in the company were reduced dramatically. The 2 percent increase was the highest level and was limited to the top 10 performers in the entire organization.

As the context changes, so too does your thinking. Most critically, the impact on your sense of satisfaction and motivation changes. With this new information, this new look, things appear much different and much brighter. While the absolute level of the salary increase has remained unchanged, its meaning and impact has changed quite a bit. You have just experienced a reframe.

The reframe cannot occur until you receive new information. That's why a leader must comes to grips with the reality that the adversity has brought forth. That's why it is so important to reflect and come to grips with what is really going on. They set the comparative base for a reframe.

Recently, *Forbes* magazine reported the establishment of a new charity, Project ALS, formed to encourage scientists and drug makers to push for a cure for ALS. ALS, commonly known as Lou Gehrig's disease, is a fatal illness where the muscles wither and paralysis ensues. The cruel irony of the disease is that while the body is slowly destroyed, the mind remains sharp. While over 25,000 Americans suffer from ALS, there is no cure and most people die within a few years. The market has simply been too small for major drug companies to invest heavily in it.

Enter four enterprising young women and Project ALS. Project ALS has prompted remarkable progress and major research advances. A cure, or at least the capacity to prolong life, may not be too far away.

What drove these women, three sisters and a close friend, to form Project ALS? Was it a keen awareness of a market niche? Was it the hope to capitalize on an untapped opportunity? No, it was crisis. Jenifer Estess initiated project ALS after she learned that she had the deadly disease. She was only 35 years old at the time. "People say this is about letting go. That's nonsense. It's about fighting." While some may have yielded or fallen, understandably, into the pit of self-pity, Jenifer chose to reframe her crisis. Her reframe did not change the reality of having ALS. But her reframe did affect her thinking, her approach to her condition, and her commitment to make a difference.[1]

Addressing Fear

Earlier in the book, we unfolded the **Paradox of Success**: *One's sense of success is enhanced by the adversities that must be overcome.* In essence, one's leadership career gains meaning and significance as adversities are met and defeated. There is a similar link between fear and challenge.

Adversity triggers concern and fear. Understandably, leaders question whether they can rise to the demands of adversity. This questioning leads to the subtle but pressing fear of failure. We have emphasized that while this fear certainly exists, it does not stifle and immobilize leaders. Instead, successful leaders are driven to conquer the fear through direct confrontation and action.

How is fear driven from the adversity experience? The answer may be surprising. Fear is not chased away. Instead, it is accepted, confronted, and placed in perspective. Fear is conquered but never eliminated. To explain, let's look more fully at the nature of fear.

Fear Threshold

Life is demanding. Leaders continually struggle with the call for change and adjustment, and with all the accompanying uncertainty and stress. They live their lives on the narrow edge between stability and chaos. For leaders, even successful leaders, there is always some level of fear present. Will this new strategy work? Will our competitors lower their price? Will the economy rebound? Will we succeed?

Leaders are not overwhelmed or consumed by this fear. In most cases, it exists as a nagging awareness. Most leaders accept some base level of fear as a natural condition of life. They deal with it, and it has little if any obvious negative impact.

But fear, like all stress, is additive. It builds and accumulates. Most people have a fear threshold. If an event or series of events heap additional fear on the base level, the fear threshold can be reached or exceeded. Suddenly, we become aware of fear, even when we have never before noticed its presence. It no longer hides behind-the-scenes. It now stands front-and-center and demands attention.

Of course, this is exactly what happens during adversity. Adversity pushes us past the threshold. Fear is activated at a level that affects how we think and behave. Fear is a complicated and highly personal emotion. Each of us experience and respond to it somewhat uniquely. In essence, we each have different fear thresholds.

Fear and Control

Despite these threshold differences, there is one theme that we all have in common. Fear affects us most dramatically when we sense a lack of control.

Here is the pattern we observed. Adversity, in and of itself, does not generate deep feelings of fear. When adversity becomes crisis, fear is activated because crisis threatens survival. Even here, it is those parts of the crisis that are beyond our control that generate fear. Reflection is so important because it helps leaders understand what they can or cannot control. As leaders search their foundations and understand their limits, their grasp of what cannot be controlled comes into sharper focus.

Consider the following example. One of our leaders noted that in most events, the presence of fear was little more than "a concern or worry." Generally, he handled these concerns with hard work and perseverance. Action and outcome overwhelmed fear. However, as he talked about a crisis involving one of his children, the fear impact changed. "I didn't know what would happen. This was all new to me. It was like being punched in the gut with no way to fight back. Yeah, I was scared." We heard similar comments about major personal health crises. We also heard accounts of business crises that followed this same pattern.

One leader who operates multiple businesses, spoke of a two-year business crisis. After an initial period of strong growth in a new high tech sector, adversity struck. "That marketplace changed. The margins plummeted just after we were trying to ramp it up into a more aggressive business plan. I didn't deal with it very well at the time. The [high tech] business was failing." He recounted how buyers with signed letters of intent backed out of the deal. "There was nothing I could do. We had to close at that point." A strong man and a successful manager, he admitted, "there was always this fear of failure in the background creeping in."

The key in this story is not the extensive, ongoing, and lengthy period of adversity that was testing this leader. The key came in his honest admission that "there was nothing I could do." Consider your own experiences with adversity. In all likelihood, you've seen this same pattern.

The Fear Reframe

Leaders handle their adversities by reframing their fear experience. Successful leaders realize that most adversities have parts that they can change. There are parts where they can make a difference. Yet, they also realize that there are parts of most adversities that they cannot control.

Successful leaders have the ability to turn loose what they cannot control. Then, they are able to concentrate their energies where they can have an impact. Turning loose is not giving up or giving in. Instead, it involves an honest appraisal. It is a decision. It is the leader's decision to put limited resources—time and attention—where they can pay the biggest dividend.

Figuring out what we are able to influence is a critical reframe. This reframe liberates and fosters challenge. There is no challenge in working like the devil to fight an adversary over which you hold no power. This only leads to a sense of futility because in spite of our good intention and our impassioned work, we will not succeed. No, challenge comes when we figure out which part of adversity we can affect and shift our focus into that realm.

Once again, note what is happening here. Fear is not eliminated. Rather, it is confronted and segmented into controllable and uncontrollable components. Successful leaders focus on the controllable because they understand that focusing on the uncontrollable is an act of desperation. As one leader commented, "Those who think they have the ability to control all that life throws their way just haven't lived enough of life." The fear reframe allows the leader to move forward and address fear.

This does not mean that leaders do not desire to control it all. They do. In fact, we all do. Some people even delude themselves into believing that they can do so. This may even work for a time. Yet, sooner or later, some test of adversity will prove the folly of this reasoning.

Turning loose that which we can't control requires three things. First, it requires an honest, personal understanding that we cannot control everything. Second, we must be confident enough to believe that what we can control will be good enough. That is a lesson of experience. Third, it comes from consciously letting go of that which cannot be controlled. Successful leaders wisely adopt, in practice, the *Serenity Prayer*: "God grant me the serenity to accept the things I cannot change, courage to change the things I can, and wisdom to know the difference."

Challenge

The leaders we interviewed were consistent. Once they captured and understood the basics of the adversity situation, adversity became a challenge. Now let's be realistic. Leaders do not lead dull lives. Generally, they are not looking for new challenges. Their plates are pretty full and the prospect of a new, unexpected challenge brings little excitement. Rather than being defeated and pulled down by the events of adversity, they are energized and focused to work through the events. The challenge is to emerge from the adversity victorious. The challenge is first, to survive, and second, to win. This process is critical, and it becomes the third piece in our rebound transformation.

There is no doubt, from our study, that the ability to approach adversity as a challenge is a decision that successful leaders make. It is a conscious and thoughtful decision. Yet, this decision is one of the most perplexing pieces of the leader rebound.

Considerable study on the nature of stress and adversity has shown, with consistency, that approaching adversity as a challenge has a positive transformational quality.[2] Further, evidence suggests that the capacity to perceive challenge in adverse events is a learned quality, affected by early pivotal experiences. We saw the same thing in our research. This capacity seems to be learned and habitual. It was shaped through early experiences and adversity encounters. Often, leaders can turn to specific examples and describe the insights and approaches gained through that experience.

As we have described, leaders first dig into themselves, finding what really counts, what is really valued, and what will truly bring meaning. Then, they seek to gain a sense of the situation facing them. They understand adversity as part of a bigger picture. This allows them to put adversity in context. It is properly framed as an interruption or just another test.

The leaders we studied recognized that they were being tested. They knew the test had critical outcomes, either for their businesses or their personal lives. They knew that their response to this test would make a difference. The test could be handled and endured, or it could be muffed. Their response, their actions, would make the difference. This was the challenge. And this is why the response to adversity became a challenge.

The Challenge Reframe

The challenge reframe is self-selective; those who were unable to reframe adversity into challenge were probably less likely to ascend to leader roles. With that in mind, our study revealed four components or themes to the challenge reframe. We will discuss each briefly.

1. Seeing Adversity as an Opportunity. It probably sounds like a well-worn cliché. Leaders see opportunities where others see problems and failures. Yet, this is exactly what we found. However, the opportunity does not simply appear magically. Rather, leaders look for opportunity. They ask, in an open and conscientious way, "Where is the opportunity in this adversity?" This is a significant reframe. They actually look for avenues of opportunity in adversity.

For a number of leaders, adversity became an opportunity to prove themselves. This was expressed in many ways. They spoke of "putting the fear behind us." They admitted to a "new energy" that was sparked, and they recognized the need to "build energy back into the organization."

They further recognized that their energies needed to address challenges rather than bemoan difficulties. One leader even commented, philosophically, that we are only given a limited amount of resources—a limited amount of time, talent, and energy. He noted that it made no sense to waste those resources. He commented that his intention and his goal was to do all he could to focus those scarce resources on challenges, not excuses. Interestingly, he spoke of this as a conscious process and decision: "I minimize the amount of energy I spend on negative thinking."

2. Appreciate the Adventure of Adversity. It may seem a bit strange or unusual, but successful leaders view adversity as an adventure. They see adversity as a piece of the leader's puzzle with unique twists and turns. Part of the satisfaction they gain from leadership comes from the unpredictable nature of adversity and the need to handle it. "Life's fun for me—even when I'm getting beat up."

Leaders also display the capacity to tackle the adversity adventure boldly and courageously. Of course, we realize that courage exists in the midst of adversity and fear. True acts of courage are played against the backdrop of adversity and fear. Successful leaders show a courageous outlook. One leader noted that you just have to "hang in there and never give up."

3. The Will to Win. Not long ago, I caught the end of a Sunday afternoon broadcast of a PGA golf tournament. Tiger Woods, in his patented fashion, had come from far behind to fight into contention and challenge the lead during the final round. As he approached the 18th green, the commentators talked about the putt Woods was about to take. The putt was long—much longer than he'd have liked. There were some tricky breaks. It was an incredibly tough putt. Even more pressing, he needed to hole the putt to move into a tie for the lead and force a playoff.

As Woods approached the green, my son remarked, "There's no way." But one look at Woods gracefully striding to that green led to my response, "Wanna bet." His face gave it away. He looked so confident—so sure. He looked as if this putt was a given. He seemed to be looking forward to the next hole. He didn't hesitate. He moved with assurance. He stroked the putt firmly, and it fell. Woods moved on and, not surprisingly won the tournament.

What struck me was that look—that confidence. It was a look of certainty. It seemed that he was saying, by an act of will, "I will not be defeated." I'd seen that look before.

Successful leaders expect to beat back the adversity. Perhaps this is because they have faced previous adversities and have been able to persevere. Since they expect to win, the process of moving through the adversity becomes exciting and motivating. As one leader noted, "I enjoy doing what can't be done."

4. Anticipating Lessons. Leaders, again drawing from their base of experiences, expect to learn from adversity. This enables them to see challenge rather than defeat in the presence of adversity.

Part of the challenge comes because successful leaders know that they will be learning and growing through the process of dealing with the adversity. "When I struggle with a problem, I know I'll learn, and I will be stronger and better." Or as another stated, "In the long run, the heavy personal decisions were strengthening." By the same token, they realize that their business will be remade or reshaped. They seemed to understand this, too, as an important developmental step.

5. Building Significance. Leaders enjoy achieving, and rebounding is another aspect of achievement. Listen to the words of one leader: "What's kept most of us going here during challenging times is that we really want to make a difference with the things that our company's all about. I always want to be involved with creating something...I like the part about doing things that can't get done, [things that] have very slim odds of getting accomplished."

There is great insight in this comment, and it is consistent with the themes developed throughout this book. Follow the logic. Leaders gain personal meaning and personal success from significance. Significance comes from making a difference. A difference is truly made under conditions of adversity where the leader's unique skills and talents are tested. Leaders know and understand this flow of events. So the grip of adversity, while carrying all the potential emotional baggage, also carries an excitement and a challenge. It is the challenge to prove oneself again and again.

———— *The Wisdom of Experience* ————

Why do some see a challenge in adversity while others are overwhelmed and defeated by adversity? We are convinced that challenge emerges from the reflective and transformational processes described earlier.

It comes from a reflection upon one's basic belief system and what really matters in life. It comes from honestly recognizing what cannot be controlled and focusing on what can be controlled. And it comes from a personal mission to make a difference in the world in which the leader lives.

The essence of the reframe is that the adverse situation is now perceived as an opportunity. It is also experienced as a challenge that motivates and energizes. The key characteristic of the reframing experience is that the leader now speaks of challenges and opportunities rather than obstacles and crises.

Nevertheless, it is the very nature of adversity to bring a person to and beyond the threshold of fear. The greater the adversity, the greater the emotional state of fear. So fear must first be managed because it can never be eliminated. In a nutshell, effective leaders do this in practice by adopting the Serenity Prayer, whether they want to call it that or not. It is a fact of life that leaders always live in a state of uncertainty. The reality is that the best-laid plans fail. And leaders know it.

Adversity is not transformed into a challenge by magic. The response has been experienced and learned over the course of a lifetime. So when a major disruption occurs, the groundwork for recovery has already been laid. Decisions must be made. And these are conscious and deliberate decisions. They are twofold: a deliberate decision to discover opportunity within adversity and the deliberate decision to move ahead with determination. These are acts of will to not only survive but to win. This attitude is manifested in a leader's posture and expressions of confidence.

Some are even capable of turning the entire episode into an adventure. This adventure is both an avenue for learning and growth and a test of their character. But this stage only appears after an earlier journey through disillusionment and reflection.

15

Courage

"I realized that I'm strong…I'm a fighter."

He had agreed to speak to a group of graduate students. These were sharp, young men and women, pursuing their tickets to organizational advancement—the MBA. There was no real need for introduction as he stood to address the group. They all knew who he was, and they knew his business. They also knew of the highly publicized issues that he and his business were facing. The details had been splashed across the business pages for the last few weeks.

After a few, brief opening comments about the general nature and demands of leadership, he opened the session for questions. This was a particular strategy he always used, and one he used quite effectively. He'd sit on the corner of the desk and respond, openly and candidly, to any questions thrown his way.

The students obliged. They were polite and considerate. Their questions were standard fare. They danced around the burning issues and questions they all wanted answered: What's going on with the business? How much of what we're reading is true? How are you dealing with all of this? What will you do next? Instead, out of respect for the visitor, these questions went unasked.

After 20 minutes of fielding these soft lobs, the leader stopped abruptly. His next comment was biting, even a bit sarcastic. "Hey, doesn't anybody here read the papers?" What ensued, over the next 75 minutes, was one of the most honest, straightforward, and insightful forays into the belly of a business crisis that any of us had experienced. It remains, through 20 years of university teaching, my most powerful class.

What intrigued me most was that the leader was willing, and even insisted, that he address the topic of the crisis. He could have skirted it, taken the easy route, and escaped unscathed. But he chose to respond. He chose to address what was pressing. He chose to step forward, knowing the possibility of personal embarrassment. He moved boldly and courageously. We learned that this courageous move, taken in the relative safety of the classroom, was reflective of the way he moved in his business, where the stakes were quite different. Consequently none of us were surprised when we saw the business bounce back and the leader lauded for his insightful handling of the situation.

A Statement of Courage

Meaning and significance are stirred and rekindled as leaders reframe adversity into challenge. We have already seen how a leader's sense of personal significance is shaken by adversity and threatened by the fear of failure. The leader emerges with new focus, renewed motivation, and an opportunity to create significance. Through perseverance the leader can find meaning and achieve success. Hope has returned, poising the leader for greatness.

However, hope is mere emotion and challenge is basic intention. Admittedly, the emotion of hope is positive, even transformational. Similarly, challenge intends to move ahead, boldly, heroically, and decisively. Yet, the leader is still only poised for greatness. There must be more.

Successful leaders not only reframe adversity into challenge, they act on it as a statement of courage. Challenge is a quality of the mind and courage is the response. Courageous leaders encounter adversity and respond with firmness and resolve.

Courage does not represent the ability to transcend, overcome, or divorce oneself from problems, troubles, or crises. Indeed, courage exists in the midst of adversity and fear. Nor is courage always bold, dramatic, and self-assured. In fact, it rarely is. Courage is always played out against the tugging emotion of apprehension and the risks of uncertainty. But, it is always played out.

The Path of Courage

The leaders we interviewed expressed courage in a number of ways. Their language was rich, instructive, and even inspirational. Let's look at some of their insights.

One leader, confronted with unexpected labor unrest and a hemorrhaging bottom line, explained that his deep adversities or crises were always coupled with a "sense of surrender." He admitted that there was a period when fleeing from or surrendering to the tough demands of adversity was an active and pressing issue.

In essence, he was experiencing the powerful tug of disillusionment and its push to give in and give up. He went on to suggest that after careful reflection, he was able to move beyond this disillusionment and sense of surrender. But, he added that there still had to be an additional response. He commented that we all play the important mind games, convincing ourselves that adversity can be met and transcended; convincing ourselves that there is a broader perspective of hope; and convincing ourselves that challenges exist within the borders of adversity. Yet, he noted that despite this mental posturing, we are still in the pit of adversity. The issues have not changed and the business outcomes have not improved.

His answer was simple and direct. "We have to leave." He didn't mean leave the business and he didn't mean leave the problems to others. For him, leaving involved moving from positive self-talk and good intention to action. It involved doing something differently. It involved making some tough decisions. As he explained, the act of leaving was the act of courage.

The act of leaving is always wrought with danger. What of the risks? Are you sure of the proper direction? What if the next step is wrong? Our leaders were consistent and clear in their response to these questions and their prescription for action. Courage does not result from a complete analysis where any risk of error or misstep is driven out. Nor does courage result from complete assurance of the proper direction, or confidence in the next step. Courage is exactly the opposite. It involves taking the next step while the risk is present, when error is a very probable outcome, and when assurance is fleeting and nebulous at best. Successful leaders are not immobilized under these conditions. They move. This is their statement of courage.

Consider the story of one of our leaders, recounting a period of crisis in the business. With the business in desperate condition, the leader noted, "For some reason, I had enough confidence, I thought I could do it [save the business]...So I took a risk...There was a challenge there, and I guess I never thought twice about it... I wasn't sure how things were going to work out...I jumped in...I thought I could do it."

Some leaders have a propensity for courage. There is nothing magical about it. This tendency is developed through experience. It grows by experiencing adversity, stepping forward, and recognizing that the lessons learned have provided new perspective and deeper insight. In essence, their courage to act has grown deeper with each subsequent response.

As another leader described a particularly trying period for his business, he noted this rebound theme. "For me, it wasn't that hard. I had confidence we were going to survive. I just didn't know how long it would take...And it has produced endurance."

Or consider these words from one of our younger leaders about dealing with the inevitable ups and downs of business and life. "I think I'm getting better at that. I think I've learned from that. And I think as you get older, you become more in tune with that..." Then, speaking of a particular crisis, he added, "You learn that all those things are always temporary. You don't really feel like going into the middle of it, ... but in the middle of it—in the valley—[You] try to be joyful in the valley because it will make you stronger. And I think that is a great perspective to have. When you are in the middle of problems, this will make me learn something, and I will be better."

In an intriguing new book, Jill Brooke talks about the life impact and learning that comes from an early tragedy. She quotes Gary Winnick, the billionaire entrepreneur who built the fiber-optics firm Global Crossing. Recalling the sudden death of his father, he noted, "No professional adversity can ever match the pain I suffered when my father died. Any obstacle thrown in my path becomes a challenge and another hurdle to climb over." He argued that the experience of that early adversity provided an invaluable lesson in courage. It taught him to take risks, and it encouraged him to keep trying and keep progressing.[1]

Some leaders note that their courage to respond has developed because of the time they spent in the reflective phase of the rebound. Given our description of reflection, this makes sense. The willingness to engage in reflection is an act of courage itself. And, it certainly fosters the courage response. Here, leaders show courage by tapping into their inner strength. In fact, this inner strength may be the defining component of courage. "I realized that I'm strong… I'm a fighter."

Some leaders express courage because they have a net for recovery. In part, that net is based on self-confidence. "If I make a mistake or go off in the wrong direction, I'll fix it." Others couple their self-reliance with a strong support network. In essence, these leaders are saying, "If I fall, I can live with it." Importantly, neither of these mechanisms reduce the risks of courage, but they do alter the perception of the downside impact if these risks are indeed realized.

For some, the net includes others. These others help build and reinforce the leader's courage to act. "They [friends and the peer network] help me reinforce how I'm looking at situations, pro and con. [They] give me an even bigger insight into the situation. . . It gives you different avenues to look at… When you open the doors and are willing to take in other people's experiences, it helps the foundation. It helps you gather more and make a stronger foundation." This leader went on to say that the network provided help, ideas, and grounding. But, most important, these networks were also there for support—no matter what. This provided a sense of security to act boldly.

There is a further dimension of courage. It may not look or even feel like courage, but it is. Sometimes, leaders take the next step because the crisis is so bad, it would be pure idiocy not to step. They realize that they cannot stay where they are. The driver is not the issue. Even if fear and chaos are the drivers, the move is always one of courage.

A Look at Courage

We were having supper together and the turn of the conversation went to character and adversity. Everett talked about placing a steel sword in the hot coals of a furnace until it glowed like gold. "And when you remove it and let it cool," he said, "it's stronger and more resistant than it was before." Nice words, nice metaphors, but, coming from Everett, these were not just pretty abstract concepts. He knew what he was talking about for he experienced more trials and tests of character in his life than most of us could bear to fantasize.

Everett Alvarez was the first American pilot shot down in Vietnam on August 5, 1964. He was not released until eight and a half years later, in 1973. His ordeal need not have been so lengthy. He could have returned home to America, to his recently married wife, to his family, and to his friends if only he would have publicly denounced his country and its involvement in Vietnam.

He would not do it. No matter how many times they beat him, tortured him, paraded him like an animal, and imprisoned him for years in solitary confinement, Everett would not yield. He would honor the Code of Conduct: "I will make no oral or written statements disloyal to my country and its allies or harmful to their cause," to which he had given his word of honor. So when Everett talked about placing a sword in hot coals to temper its steel, I knew I was listening to someone whose character was indeed forged in the cauldron of adversity.

He was the first captured pilot held prisoner of war in Vietnam and the last to be released. He lived alone for years in a 7x7-foot cement cell, in a complex (Hanoi Hilton) reeking of excrement, alone, with rats and vermin as company. His only breaks were for torture. Naturally, the question arises: How did he do it?

"I was not special. If I could do it, so could others with a decent code of conduct as a guide."[2] He says simply that it was his "belief in all the intrinsic values which are inherent in just being an American" that gave him strength. Everett defines those beliefs as his duty to God, his country, and to his fellow man.

There were opportunities for better food, early release, and freedom from torture if he would only collaborate with the enemy. During the course of the war 12 or so POWs out of over 500 did collaborate; one became an assistant jailer for the North Vietnamese while others got an early release back to the USA. But the majority of POWs honored Article III of the Code of Conduct: "I will accept neither parole nor special favors from the enemy."

Everett has shared his experiences with the American public.[3] Although he responded to Larry King's question of what is it like to be shot down with the humorous quip: "It tends to ruin your day," he talks candidly about his fear and the loss of control over his life. When his plane started falling out of the sky he was "scared right down to the socks." When he got captured, his fears ranged from being castrated, to other forms of torture, to outright execution. Yet, in the face of daily uncertainties and ongoing adversities he talked about turning them into challenges and opportunities!

Mental control was something no one could take away from him. And so he exercised control over what he thought and how he thought about it. He would concentrate on the things he could control and not on what he could not, such as what was happening to his family and newly married wife.

When tortured to give up his faith in America and to betray his comrades, he drew upon his basic values and beliefs. That was the source of his courage. There were, as he said, higher goods and values than mere self-preservation. Although he might break— "cry uncle"—under the pain of physical torture, as did all POWs who were tortured, and sign a document, this was only done after hours and even days of excruciating pain, starvation, and beatings. His captors had to work to get it out of him, bringing him to the point of death or permanent physical disability.

The enemy tried to use him, a Mexican-American, and an African-American Air Force pilot, Fred Cherry, as oppressed minorities in America to split the group. It didn't work. They were Americans first, and proud of their country.

Everett defines courage as the willingness to risk self-destruction in obedience to a goal more important than oneself. For him, it was summarized in the first part of his Boy Scout Oath taken as a teenager: "On my honor I will do my best to do my duty to God and to Country." This is not the kind of conversation one hears these days.

He didn't do it alone. It was the support of the community of prisoners that helped each one bear their torture. Through an elaborate communication system, their code was that each one would bear as much torture as he could physically stand before being forced to sign a propaganda statement. Every man had a breaking point. It would come sooner or later to everyone. Those that didn't, died.

It was humiliating to give up in screaming pain and tears, but support, communicated by taps on the walls came back saying it's OK, you did the best you could do. And so each returned, broken, to his cell. Yet he and his fellow tortured POWs still honored the code by refusing any special deals, privileges, or release. Each returned to wait. For it would happen again; they just didn't know when.

Everett Alvarez refused to allow the crisis he faced for over eight years to define him. By an act of spirit and will, he fought the damning consequences of surrendering to disillusionment. He reframed his daily adversities into challenges or testimonies of honor to the country he loved. Clearly, he is a man of courage.

Yet his courage was more than a statement of hope. While always present, hope was a distant image. Similarly, his courage was more than a statement of challenge. Existence was challenge enough. Alvarez's courage was in what he did. His courage was in each small, yet significant, action he forced himself to make. He showed courage when he drove himself to adhere to a routine. He showed courage when he sought and provided support through the ponderous "tapping" regimen that became a source of both communication and strength. He showed courage when he decided to keep going and tolerate as much as he could when the pressures to give in were overwhelming. Always uncertain and unsure and laden with risk, these acts were his bullets of courage.

The Wisdom of Experience

Courage is an action. It is intentional. It is always played against the hand of adversity. Courageous acts are rarely smooth and collected. Courageous acts, more typically, are uncertain and anxious.

Successful leaders move beyond the transforming potential of challenge. They step forward and act. That step, that action, is a statement of courage. Courage is incremental and self-perpetuating. The initial acts of courage foster further steps. Successful leaders, each with their own unique stories, are truly examples of courage under fire.

In the process of reframing adversity into challenge, the passion for significance, is rekindled. The driving desire to make a difference also becomes a source of courage to take action, to endure uncertainty with confidence, and to brave risk.

Courage and confidence are just two sides of the same coin. Action and emotion are wedded in one act. Successful leaders know that they will win-out. They will endure because they are on a mission that is greater than they are. Yet this is never pure hubris, for our leaders all recognized that their achievements were also the result of the support, advice, and assistance they received from others.

16

Staying the Course

"Do what needs to be done day to day."

In the recent television series *Betting It All*, successful entre-
preneurs from the high tech field discussed how they faced
and survived adversities brought on by the recent hard times
bombarding their industry. T.J. Rogers, CEO of Cypress
Semiconductor, spoke of the need to persevere and do the best
you can, while trying to sort out and deal with the shifts and
challenges of the last few years. He seemed to realize that his
"stay the course" actions brought a sense of stability to the business during these trying periods. His formula was direct, "You
do the best job you can do. You convince yourself that you're
managing competently, and you go home and let it slide." He
realized that while you may move only one small step at a time,
you still must keep moving.[1]

Over half a century ago, Winston Churchill boldly said, "If you
are going through hell, keep going." With perhaps less flair, but
certainly no less conviction, the words of the leaders we interviewed mirrored those of the great statesman, "You may never
really know what to do. You keep doing things until you find the
key. You stick to the principles and just keep going. You know this
is the next step to take. Sometimes you make little progress.
Sometimes you have to go back. . . Try things. Most of them may
fail. But a couple of them work. You keep trying things."

The Challenge of Staying the Course

The experience of adversity or crisis always carries competing demands. While disillusionment, introspection, and reflection are taking place, the leader has to keep doing the business of the business. And while the leader continues with business, he struggles to figure out exactly what has occurred, why, and how actions can be adjusted to deal with the current events.

It would be highly therapeutic if the leader could somehow withdraw for a while; the leader could study, ponder, reflect, and return to organizational life after everything was worked out. While this method may seem ideal, it is, of course, unrealistic. Such luxury rarely exists. Instead, leaders have to keep going, moving through the adversity. This is one of the toughest and most demanding acts the leader must endure under adversity. So before moving on to phase three, the adjustment, let's look at how our leaders maintained themselves during the rebound process.

Our leaders expressed tenacity in even their most basic phrases. "Stay busy." "Charge on." "Keep going." "Do what needs to be done day-to-day." These leaders knew that even while trying to dissect and decipher the messages and revelations of adversity, one had to keep plugging away. In short, they were doing their best to keep their heads above the water during a time of stress.

The Action and the Impulse

This basic message of staying the course may seem simple, but it is one of the defining statements of the leader rebound. It involves a series of actions whose impact is often missed. To all but a few select insiders, it may appear that all is progressing as it always has. The reality is that leaders are charging on even when their course has become blurred and their steps are halting and uncertain.

As we have described in the previous chapters, the leader has progressed through confusion, disillusionment, anger, and thoughtful reflection. But the leader's world is far from certain. Things are not yet sorted out. Trauma and internal uncertainty have not been overcome. Questions abound, and clear answers seem far in the distance.

Yet the leaders know, perhaps instinctively, that they cannot break and business must proceed. As T. J. Rogers recognized in our opening profile, the leader must project stability. Somehow, successful leaders maintain the course and keep pressing on. All the while they know that their present course may need to be changed and their steps may need to be retraced. They persevere, even in the face of uncertainty and wavering control.

Listen to the perspective of a bright, dynamic CEO recounting an extended market downturn and a prolonged period of business crisis. "I came into this business . . . right at the beginning of the deep recession. And this business and the climate we operated in got worse every day. Every single day for two years, it was worse every single day. . . Life got worse every day. . . It was not an issue of what are you going to do with your resources and how are we going to put them to improve the business. It was an issue of what are you going to do with your resources to keep the business surviving? It was interesting, that is not a concept you learn in school . . I learned finance by fire . . . and that helped mold me."

When pressed to explain how he kept going, this leader's response was immediate and clear. "There is no substitute for hard work. My favorite quote, whether you like him or not, is a quote from George S. Patton. I've operated under this all my life. 'A good plan executed now is better than a perfect plan executed next week.' It's true. I mean if you're in a responsible position, just dig in and do it."

Successful leaders understand that they have no options. The business must proceed. They do what makes sense, knowing that the path will probably be corrected once everything is sorted out and greater clarity is gained. But, they accept no other alternative. They do not withdraw from the business. Rather, they are a visible presence. They stay. They do the work. They progress as best they can.

The same response was present for family-related problems. One leader talked of a family crisis involving one of his children. "I was in a fog. It was all surreal. I was going through the motions. I guess I was doing what needed to be done. I'd go to work early, go to the hospital, go back to work, then back to the hospital. At night, I just felt empty and helpless, but I knew I had to get up and do it all again tomorrow." Or consider these comments, "All perspective had suddenly changed. The business wasn't the top priority, but I knew I had to keep working the business. I had responsibilities."

The same pattern of perseverance, to a large extent, remains for most personal problems. Except for extreme health crises, when leaders were forced to withdraw, the leaders we interviewed attempted to stay the course. One leader, reflecting on his personal health problems, admitted that it was hard to stay focused on the business at hand when "your own mortality was suddenly drawn into question." Yet, he maintained his business priorities. Largely, leaders realized that this was the wrong time to make a dramatic shift in the business. Emotions were running too high.

Andy Grove, mentioned earlier, illustrates this dynamic perfectly. He set blocks of time aside each day to learn about prostate cancer, do research, and reflect on the various options available to him. All the while, he kept right on with the daily issues of the Intel business right up and into the evening before his surgical implant radiation began the following morning. As Grove illustrates, there are many aspects to living life. When a disruption strikes one part, individuals must protect the other aspects of life so that their entire life does not become immobilized. This is the strategy of compartmentalization. A failure to use it is a sure-fire recipe for disaster.

How to Persevere

How do successful leaders persevere through adversity? Admittedly, our group had difficulty explaining how. We pressed them, and even did more digging in follow-up interviews designed to probe this arena further. We found three keys: The Big Picture, Time, and Operating on Principle.

1. The Big Picture. First, leaders are able to persevere because they understand, through personal experience, the bigger picture. We have talked of this earlier, but it bears repeating. Since successful leaders know that adversity is merely an interruption or break in their pattern of success, they recognize that the down period is only temporary. Even in the face of adversity, leaders seem to know that eventually the bigger picture will emerge.

Return again to T. J. Rogers from Cypress Semiconductor. He put his current business adversity in perspective by noting that in his 18 years at Cypress he'd been through two yearlong recessions. "...People know that I'm in for the long haul." He understood the periodic ups and downs of the market and the need to act in the long-term interests of his shareholders.[2] He focused more on the big picture than the pressing snapshots of the moment.

2. Time. Leaders realize that healing the wounds of adversity takes time. They recognize that, with time, adversity will pass and a new future will emerge. They understand the altering effect of time. One leader commented on this theme in poetic fashion, "You can see the sunshine, but until you get past the conflict, you don't see the brightness of day."

This perspective, too, has been gained through experience. Leaders have seen this pattern, they have felt depression, and they have learned that it will eventually pass. They also recognize that if they keep plugging away, things will eventually become clearer and brighter.

3. Operating on Principle. We have commented on how important it is for leaders to stay the course, to keep going even as they are in the midst of their adversity struggles. We have asked how this is done. The answer we heard most often: "When [you're] down, you operate on principle."

That may sound broad and even confusing, but to our leaders it was simple. If the business was built on customer service, actions that moved the business in that direction were continued. If the business stressed quality, actions consistent with quality moves were continued. This was a time to continue the basics.

Many of our leaders stressed a personal principle: projecting a "can-do" attitude, even during adversity. These leaders realized that their mood affected others, which in turn could easily affect the adversity. This principle was stated most clearly by the executive who candidly shared, "I don't have the luxury to walk in that front door in a bad mood. Because when I walk in the front door in a bad mood, I drag everyone else down. . . I have probably conditioned myself to walk in that door and try to be up. . . If people see me that way, then hopefully they will realize that is the tone we want to set for the organization, and they will follow through."

The Wisdom of Experience

Life goes on. Successful leaders make sure they keep up with the demands of daily business and life amidst the rebound process. They have the capacity to work and switch channels as the situation demands. This ability to compartmentalize is one of their key tactics employed during adverse times.

THE ADVERSITY CHALLENGE

Perseverance is the required virtue throughout any crisis. Leaders persevere because they are able to place adversity within its proper context. Furthermore, leaders do not pass on their anxiety, fears, and desperation to their followers. They proceed with a demeanor of confidence that spreads throughout the organization. Even if they don't feel it, they act as if they do because their confidence is rooted in their commitment to accept the challenge of adversity and to work through it.

17

Making Adjustments

"Focus more on what you can get done than on what can go wrong."

One leader recalled mentoring a relatively young employee who had been with the business about five years. The young man was struggling with his future and his career direction. The leader noted that the young man "had all the talent in the world," but he still could not decide whether he wanted to go through a major managerial training program that the company had offered to him. To a large extent, the nature of his career with the company was tied to that decision.

The leader noted that the young man did not mind the hard work that would be involved. "But he had a fear of failure, and he said [he was] not sure that he really wanted to manage." The young man's vacillation and uncertainty added stress to a decision long overdue.

The leader addressed the young man and cut to the heart of the matter: "This is not about the work. This is not about the future. This is about your inability to make a decision." He then mentioned a senior executive they both knew and respected: "I've watched him make decisions. Do you know how he makes a decision?" The employee replied, "Well I bet he studies it." "Nope, he flips a coin." And standing there, the leader pulled out a coin and said, "You know what we're going to do? Flip it, and you ought to do whatever the coin says you ought to do. Because you need to go and make a decision." And the young man asked, "What if I'm wrong?" His mentor replied, "You know what? If you're wrong, just flip it again. . . The key is make the decision."

At some point, leaders need to decide to act, to change, and to adjust. These adjustments can be both personal and situational. Personal adjustments involve beliefs, tendencies, styles, and habits and require a change in the leader's thinking and actions. Situational adjustments deal with the realm of decision-making and implementation. Situational adjustments require a plan of action to address the conditions arising from adversity. Generally, personal adjustments must precede situational adjustments. Not surprisingly, for most of us, personal adjustments are far more difficult to understand and put in place.

The organizational world is comprised of many managers and leaders who face adversity but never step up and make the necessary personal adjustments. There are many reasons for this failure. Self-confrontation is never easy, and adjustments indicate in clear terms that present patterns are not acceptable. Adjustment is an admission that some aspect of the leader's own thinking or behavior is suspect. Furthermore, adjustment requires change. Most executives are already overwhelmed with demands; change is the last thing they want. It is easy to understand their reluctance to assume personal responsibility and adjust.

For many leaders, analyzing a competitive business situation and developing strategies for addressing pressing business demands is relatively easy. However, making the necessary personal adjustments is not. At times, even good and talented leaders fight this every inch of the way and with every ounce of their being.

Successful leaders break this pattern. Once they have analyzed the situation, successful leaders step forward and make needed personal adjustments. The rebound is no longer merely a mental activity; now, the leader must do things differently based on what has been learned. These acts are never easy and, as noted earlier, are tests of courage. In fact, the act of adjustment defines the outcome of the adversity encounter. This is the heart of the leader rebound.

Making an Adjustment

Today's business mantra emphasizes action. Faced with uncertainty and turmoil, leaders need to act. Staying put is a surefire way to assure that you will lose ground, particularly in an environment of intensifying competitive strength. We are reminded of the old adage, "Don't just stand there, do something."

Doing something without the proper reflection can be chaotic and unproductive. However, once reflection has occurred, successful leaders "do something," and, more importantly, they "do something differently." They step up and make an adjustment.

Even if they may not be absolutely certain about where to go or how to act, adversity has taught them where they should not go and how they should not act. Rather than perpetuate a failing pattern, they make adjustments, knowing that the exact path out is foggy. As one leader commented, "You've got to do something— make a change. There's no point crying about adversity if you're not willing to make an adjustment."

Adjusted Thinking

The leaders talked at length about adjusting their thinking, their focus, and their mindset. They realized, clearly, that there are times when changing the pattern of thinking is necessary and healthy. Adversity can be trying and even depressing. Anger can take over. It's easy to get caught in a downward spiral of self-pity and negative thinking.

Successful leaders are aware of these potential pitfalls, and they refuse to slip over the edge. Is this merely positive self-talk? Are these mind games? Probably, but the adjustment has critical psychological merit. Adjusted thinking becomes a matter of focus. "Sometimes I have to change the way I'm thinking." "Don't dwell on failures too long." Or consider these words of wisdom. "Focus more on what you can get done than on what can go wrong."

Internal Consistency

Prompted by adversity, leaders reflect on what brought them personal significance and what is really important for them. They ask the critical question "What really counts?" Our leaders found the answers to this personal reflection to be revealing and quite meaningful, but the answers usually required a closer look and reconnection with ones' core foundations and values.

Sometimes, in the grasp of adversity, leaders recognized that their behavior is simply not in line with these foundations and values. There is a disconnect between what is important and what is actually done. Being aware of this gap creates an uncomfortable tension. An adjustment is required to close the gap. In the absence of a clear direction, successful leaders make adjustments consistent with their values and principles.

One leader named his set of values and principles "that sense of personal vision." He said that "personal vision doesn't change. It can't waiver." Consider the story of one high-flying leader, thrown off course by the trauma of adversity. The leader admitted to being a workaholic, citing many long, pressure-packed workdays. "I had many a night where I would just fall asleep with paper on my face, literally." While the business prospered, family and personal health suffered. Adversity forced this leader to consider what really mattered, and that meant a balance between family and career. An adjustment was needed. Slowly, some of the internal reins of the business were relinquished. The business, by design, became less consuming. The leader noted a need to be home more, to "work smart...not until I drop from exhaustion." "I still love it [the work] obviously. I'm still working more than eight hours a day, but I'm not working 18 hours a day."

Adjustment begins when leaders adjust their lives and their business actions to reflect their answer to the question "What really matters?" Let's consider some common adjustments. While certainly not an exhaustive list, these represent the key themes revealed through our leader interviews.

Handling Personal Mistakes

The leaders we interviewed spoke at length about how they made adjustments to handle mistakes they had committed. Their message was consistent, as was the suggested pattern of adjustment.

First, leaders need to recognize that they have made a mistake. Successful leaders do not look for excuses, and they do not look for scapegoats. Rather they recognize the need to be honest enough to admit they have made a mistake. As one leader stated, "You have to admit the mistake to yourself." Interestingly, this admission is not really a matter of assigning blame; it is a matter of accepting responsibility.

Once the leaders make this personal admission, they move to the second step: admitting their mistakes to the key people who must deal with its impact. While there may be a tendency to shy from this step, our leaders were firm. "Admit you blew it." "Don't sugarcoat it."

The behavioral logic of this second step is important. Most people know who is responsible for the mistake anyway. Failing to admit to the mistake is often viewed as a sign of weakness and a lack of self-confidence. It also appears to others that the leader is placing personal ego ahead of what makes sense for the business. Admitting the mistake is a statement of credibility, openness, and trust.

The third step is offering apologies when necessary. Any time the mistake affects other people in a negative way, an apology is needed. In fact, an apology can be a powerful remedial event if it's handled properly. A sincere apology may be as simple as, "I'm sorry. I shouldn't have done that." The apology should be coupled with a statement of intent to make changes that will remedy the mistake.

Finally, leaders must see that the mistake is fixed. As one leader said, "If you tear something up or something doesn't work, fix it." Successful leaders recognize that this step is really the key. Analysis, admission, and apology provide a base, but correcting mistakes is what makes the difference.

Making Business Adjustments

Business adjustments are often complex, and often contain a great deal of emotional involvement. While they differ from personal adjustments, the approach to business adjustments is probably a bit closer to the leaders' comfort zone.

When faced with a business problem, our leaders asked, "What is the immediate point of corrective action?" While this may seem to be a straightforward issue, this point has considerable depth. Although they understood the importance of a broad or comprehensive strategic approach, these leaders recognized that certain pressing issues had to be addressed immediately in order to move beyond adversity and progress. This was especially true during crisis when survival was being threatened. Some adjustments needed to be made now, today.

Once leaders are able to identify the problems, they move quickly to develop a plan of action and adjustment for moving through the adversity. Now this should come as no surprise. Leaders are planners. They lay out plans, and they work their plans. They are applying methods that work in business situations to their rebound situation. Many accept the underlying truth that "the best way to bounce back is to get an action plan." As one leader stated, "Get into a 'do it' mode. Pour yourself into addressing the challenge."

Consider the following example. Gordon Bethune took the leadership reins at Continental Airlines in 1994. In the years immediately preceding his appointment, Continental, by any objective measure, had the worst track record among the nation's biggest airlines. The company had declared Chapter 11 bankruptcy twice in the previous decade. With the company's stock at rock bottom and employee morale in the doldrums, the only thing approaching record levels was customer complaints.

Getting the business back on track was a daunting task, but one that was successfully achieved. Bethune, commenting on how the turnaround was accomplished stated, "It has to do with not just identifying strategies but actually doing something to solve problems."[1]

Handling People Issues

We asked our interviewees to talk about the aspects of their careers that had been the most dissatisfying or frustrating. With few exceptions, one theme prevailed: people. Overwhelmingly, personnel matters were mentioned. These experiences ranged from feeling betrayed by a trusted colleague to intractable personal conflicts between key and valued managers. They included figuring out tough motivational problems to dispensing disciplinary actions. Not surprisingly, having to fire someone, particularly a member of management, was listed as the toughest decision.

Given the intensity of this theme, it is probably no surprise that dealing with people issues were some of the more trying adjustments that our leaders had to make. They said it was important to address people issues with honesty and adhere to principle. They also mentioned that this must be done in a timely manner. People issues, if not handled promptly and decisively, can spread discontent and feelings of inequity throughout an organization.

Incremental Steps

All adversities differ. Some are inconveniences while others are full-blown crises. We realize that the type and depth of adversity affect the nature of adjustment. However, most leaders travel through adversity by making steady, incremental steps. Rarely is the path clear enough that a grand step or speedy run through the adversity can be taken. Leaders make progress, but that progress evolves over time.

Most adversities do not appear overnight, full-blown, in all their ugly color. By the same token, most cannot be removed with a single wave of a magic wand. If adversities take time to build, they will usually take time to resolve. One must attack the issues, methodically and steadily. As one seasoned leader recognized, "Keep moving up the stairs little steps at a time."

The adversity plan emerges over time. Although leaders develop a plan of action and adjustment, they realize that the plan itself will need adjustment as they progress through the adversity. They accept this reality. They don't refrain from working the plan simply because all the details have not yet fallen into place.

One senior leader talked at length about this emerging process. He noted that you have to get a plan, use the plan, but be careful to be flexible as new signals and evidence become apparent. "Choose a direction. If you don't select the best direction—that's all right. Learn from that. Pick a better direction." Another leader commented, "Go out and make a decision. The key is the decision. You can change it tomorrow."

The Dual Definition

Successful leaders have the ability to redefine the moment's issue and keep the larger picture in view at the same time. This ability to see the big picture is important. While they are putting out fires and taking immediate corrective action, they are framing and adjusting their broader strategy. In short, they are defining both the immediate issue and the larger frame of activities.

Moving On

Successful leaders are quick to correct mistakes, and they are quick to move on. This is part of their rebound nature. Catch their reasoning: Mistakes happen; they are part of maturing. Leaders refuse to dwell on mistakes or let mistakes drag them down. They focus on adjustment and correction. They recognize the mistake and then move to finding a strategy to build success. Leaders learn from the mistake, and they vow to not make that same mistake again—"Don't trip on it again." Leaders move on and they move ahead.

To a large extent, our leaders approached all adversities from this framework: Handle it as best you can and move on. No matter how traumatic an event or how disastrous a decision, these leaders exhibited the capacity to adjust and not become entrapped by the adversity. They said it well: "Don't dwell on failures too long. Focus more on what you can get done than on what can go wrong."

The Wisdom of Experience

In adversity, adjustments must be made, even when you don't yet have perfect information, total clarity of direction, and certainty of approach. In fact, during adversity and crisis, waiting to make the ideal adjustment will most likely block you from taking needed action at all.

Successful leaders make the best adjustments that they can at a given moment. The adage of "he who hesitates is lost" applies here. Once leaders have received necessary information, listened to advice, and reflected on the options, they need to act. Effective leaders know that even if their actions turn out badly, they have the inner resources to recover and change directions.

Adjustments fall into one of two categories—personal and situational. Personal adjustments require leaders to change their thinking. Situational adjustments require a plan of action or series of steps to address the effects of adversity. In both categories, leaders must make real changes, and this requires courage.

Most adjustments are incremental and emerging. Leaders understand that their adjustments will evolve and change as further evidence is attained. Leaders create plans of action as a way of forming better plans of action as new realities emerge.

THE LESSONS
OF EXPERIENCE

18

The Adversity Check

"When the pressure is on . . . do I like what I see?"

At a recent workshop, we worked with group of young managers on how to deal with problem people. We asked the participants to identify a specific example, if they had one. Rarely does this activity miss in generating some interesting stories and capturing the full attention of the audience.

A young woman, in her first management position, spoke first. She started guardedly. But soon her emotions took hold. Her issue was not with a subordinate, but with a peer. "He's awful. When anything goes wrong, he goes ballistic." As we probed a bit, she revealed that he was talented and performed adequately, although "not nearly as good as he thinks he is." We asked what she meant by the phrase, "he goes ballistic." "Well, it varies. Sometimes, he looks for a scapegoat. A problem is never his fault. He finds someone to blame. If it's you, he belittles you. Sometimes, it's even more intense. He'll yell and scream—just go ballistic."

We asked the next logical question. How has this behavior been addressed? What has his boss done? "Oh, he gets talked to when one of these tirades occurs. He gets that hurt puppy-dog look and says he's sorry. It's the pressure. It won't happen again. And that works for a little while until the next problem comes along."

Then, with a contemplative expression, she asked for an opinion. "He says it's the pressure, that he's not really like that. But to me, he just doesn't seem like a nice person. What do you think?" We had little doubt.

The real leader is revealed in adversity. Your actions under adversity present a picture of the real leader that you are. Take a look at yourself as a leader. Look carefully. Look non-defensively, if you can, and see what other people see.

You may not like all that is revealed. You may find reasons to dismiss the leader you see. You may argue, "But that's not really me. I'm not that angry and manipulative. I really don't have that short fuse that they say I do. I don't really run roughshod over others. I'm really in this for my people, not my own ego and my own advancement." You may argue that it's the pressure or the current crisis. You may truly believe that what's happened during this recent adversity has made you something that you're not.

If this pattern of thought looks at all familiar, stop! Face the facts and face them honestly. We are convinced that your real leadership is not thrown off base by crisis. Instead, during crisis, the mask is discarded. In crisis, your true colors shine forth. Your real leadership is revealed through adversity.

Espoused and Real Leaders

Edgar Schein has done pioneering work in the area of organizational culture. Schein's writings are instructive, and they are provocative.[1] Among the keys to understanding culture, Schein points out that there is a huge difference between the "espoused culture" and the "enacted or real culture." The espoused culture is made up of those beliefs and values that the organization's leaders contend count. The real culture is made up of those beliefs and values that are actually put into practice. They are the beliefs and values that are reinforced through organizational practices and rewards.

Schein's ideas have been simplified by the often-recited organizational question, "Do you walk the talk?" Of course, we understand the implication of this question. People typically focus their attention more toward the walk—the action—than the talk.

On an individual scale, leaders are seen for what they espouse. Leaders tell us what they believe in, what they value, how they intend to deal with people, and what sort of practices, styles, and decision processes make sense to them. These expressions define the espoused leader.

But there is also a real leader. Here, intention is less important than action. Dramatic pronouncements are less important than delivery. What the leader actually does provides the testimony. The leader's words and behavior reveal the values, beliefs, and practices that represent the real leader. The real leader is seen in the walk.

A Snapshot of the Real Leader

Those who study culture contend that one of the best ways to understand the real culture of an organization is to see what happens during crisis. It is then that the real culture shines through most clearly.

The following example that has gained recent press illustrates this well. Some businesses, despite feeling pressed to shave costs, have made a conscious decision to steer away from the downsizing route. In part, they contend that downsizing is inconsistent with the open and supportive cultures that they so carefully nourished. Some companies have even obtained voluntary salary reductions from their people in exchange for a commitment to retain more jobs. These are powerful cultural statements.

It is easy to say we support people—it is tougher to prove it, creatively, when the pressure is on. People believe the values expressed during difficult times reflect what really is important. This is the real culture.

Again, there is an analogous message for leaders. Throughout this book, we have addressed adversity as both a condition of life and a test of the leader's mettle. Adversity tests leaders' character. Their true colors come forth. Leaders can espouse anything. They can espouse a winning message that's in sync with the latest thinking or the most current leadership fad. But, what do they do when the pressure is on? What do they do when confronted with the tests of adversity? Actions under fire indicate the real leader residing beneath the surface. It is the actions under adversity that provide a descriptive snapshot of the real leader.

Return to the manager described in the opening of this chapter. Granted, human behavior is complex, but coworkers saw him break into angry tirades at the first hint of adversity, and that was the manager they had to address. Regardless of the causes or foundations, that was the real manager.

Consider another common example. Many leaders contend that they care about their people. They utter a standard organization statement, that "our people are our most important asset." But do they prove it? In our consulting activities, we have met with many leaders. We spend time discussing their units and issues affecting the units. We talk with them about how they lead. We gain a sense of how they think they behave as leaders. Then we meet with their direct reports and peers—people who see and deal with them everyday. They've seen them during good times. And, more critically, they have seen them during the rough times. Often, the leader they talk about is not the same leader we encountered. We have seen the cool and collected presence. They have seen the leader when the heat was on.

Recently during a leadership training session, we worked with a middle-aged manager who was struggling on the job. We surmised that he had probably been sent to the workshop as part of a final chance to save what had once been a promising career. A man of considerable technical competence, he was ruthless in his patterns of interactions. He was a poster child of the talented, but abrasive manager. Colleagues stayed out of his way. Peers tried to make sure that they shared no team assignments. His employees, to a large extent, feared him. His career was in a free fall, and it had been for over a year.

While he accepted the feedback that others had provided, he offered an explanation. There had been a series of adversities over the past year. One had involved his family. Another had revolved around his relationship with a superior. These adversities made sense, and they were real. These adversities, he contended, explained the behavior that others had seen. He argued that his unfortunate and admittedly dysfunctional behavior came from these adversities.

There was probably some merit to this argument. Even those in his business, aware of some of his recent difficulties, conceded that these problems probably played some role. But they went on to explain that his behavior over the past year was not really a departure from the past. Adversity had merely brought it out more clearly. Now his behavior problems were more intense. But, they asserted, the basic pattern had not changed.

The Adversity Check

Adversity is a wonderful mirror for viewing the real leader. It reveals the leader others have seen more often than you suspect. Too often the adversity mirror reflects a less attractive, less approachable leader. It's important to take a hard and objective look into that mirror.

Let's put you to work by looking at a common adversity—interpersonal conflict. Think of a recent conflict involving you and another person. This could be related to work, family, or any social group. Pick a conflict that meets two conditions. First, you must be one of the principal parties in the conflict. You must be involved and invested in the conflict, not simply a third party or casual observer. Second, choose a conflict that you find particularly disturbing. No soft lobs here. Pick a conflict that has consequence to you. Now, see the conflict as it unfolds. What is the setting? Who is present? What's being said? What nonverbal messages are being sent? Try to capture a sense of everything going on.

Now, painful as that may have been, step back and do some analysis. Why did this conflict occur? Be honest. Did the other party do something bothersome? Did they fail to follow through on a commitment? What about you? This is not a matter of being factual. It's not a matter of absolute right and wrong. It's a matter of recognizing and defining your impressions. Be able to say, "This is why I think the conflict is there."

Now, let's move to the next level. When you were in the midst of the conflict, how did you feel? Concentrate on specific feelings or emotions. Were you angry, frustrated, confused, or sad? Name the emotions that were present as best you can.

Now, a final query: How did you act? Again, look at your behavior as objectively as you can. There is no need to explain or justify. Simply look at what you did. Now evaluate how effective was your response?

If you have followed this path, you have been involved in an adversity check. Our guess is the pattern and outcomes you have uncovered here are not atypical. We encourage you to tune into what is revealed. Is that person in the mirror of the adversity check the real you?

———————— *The Wisdom of Experience* ————————

Organizational beliefs and values are manifested each day by what the leader does, and not by official pronouncements and written statements. When the organization and its leaders are under pressure, the real values are revealed. The true character of the leader and of the organization will either shine or darken.

There are plenty of written statements of corporate values and beliefs regarding employees and customers. They look nice on the walls of the main lobby. But few people ever read them. However, everyone in the organization knows the true corporate values because they experience them. The true values are set by the behavior of the senior leaders in the corporation. This is the only language that employees and customers hear.

The throes of adversity reveal the leader's true character. Answer these questions honestly: "When the pressure is on, how do I comport myself? Do I like what I see? Do others like what they see? And if not, what am I going to do about it?"

19

What We Become

"I don't know... but after a few knocks, you do look at things differently."

I'm different. I've changed a lot... and I've probably changed the most in the last few years [a period of intense adversity]. I think I'm less intense, less intimidating. I take things in stride better. I don't get worked up and worried about every issue—every problem. Don't get me wrong. I'm competitive—always have been—in sports and on the job. I don't want to loose that drive. But, I'm more focused. I believe in taking care of the details, but I don't obsess over them like I used to do. I've heard people say that I've mellowed. I don't know... but after a few knocks, you do look at things differently."

As captured in the comments above, leadership is an ongoing learning process. Most of you will recognize that each leadership experience taught you new lessons that have shaped what you are today. Some of those lessons reinforced what you already knew, believed, and practiced. These lessons provided assurance and confidence. Other lessons caused you to question and stretch, tweaking and adjusting to carefully hone your leader skills. And some of the lessons were dramatic, challenging and shook your foundations. These lessons altered your thinking and practices. You too are a work in progress.

175

This book has been about that progress. We have discussed change and transformation and explored, with considerable detail, the transformations that come from adversity and crisis. Our leader interviews uncovered moving stories of how the touch of adversity shaped successful leaders. With the humility of reflection and the confidence gained through endurance, each leader could truly say, "I'm different."

How had they been transformed? What's different today because of the experience? Through the tests of adversity, what had they become? To conclude our interviews, we asked "what have you become?" The philosophical tone of this question caught some leaders off guard. Yet, their answers revealed straightforward and profound patterns.

The responses to this question were as complex and filled with nuance as the personalities we interviewed. Any attempt to categorize and explain such complexity loses some of the personal impact. Despite these cautions, what remains is highly instructive.

Ten Lessons

We present 10 lessons our leaders learned as products of their adversity experiences.

Lesson 1—Managing Perceptions of Adversity. We all know that there is a difference between the world of perception and the world of reality. What we observe and how we interpret what we observe may differ from what really is. Yet, most of us are also aware of another psychological truism. Your perception is your reality, and that perceived reality drives your feelings and actions.

As one of our leaders wisely stated, "I start every day thinking it's going to be a good day because I know plenty of people who start every day thinking it's going to be a bad day. And you know what? They're going to be right."

Successful leaders understand the value of managing their personal perception of adversity. They know they have a choice. They can view adversity as a debilitating and crushing event, or they can see adversity as an interruption, a detour on the road to success. In either case, successful leaders realize their choice will affect their reality.

The experience of adversity helps leaders gain perspective. They learn to see the big picture and accept that it will always be a bit murky and out of focus. They learn to take the highs and lows for what they are—points in time. They learn to commit themselves to not get too low. They learn to avoid a line of action that will likely propel a downward spiral. They learn that both the highs and lows will shift and return again. "You learn to relegate the ups and downs to their proper position." "You never know the full picture." These leaders showed us that the experiences of adversity, properly approached, helped them become fuller and richer people.

Lesson 2—Know Yourself. Socrates said the unexamined life was not worth living. Our leaders learned this lesson. They emerged from the trials of adversity convinced of the importance of self-examination. "You've got to know yourself before you can lead others." "Understand yourself. More than anything else, understand yourself." "You learn that you've got to treat yourself with respect."

It appears that when you honestly know yourself, you develop self-confidence—honest and realistic confidence. "I recognize that I'm not infallible. I'm not some sort of super-person. I have skills, and I believe I can get it done. Generally, I have confidence in myself and believe I can accomplish what I set out to do."

Many of our leaders acquired the ability to "not take myself so seriously." "You're part of the picture—only a part." They learned the importance of balance in all aspects of life. "Maintain a balance in your life...and don't let any one facet of life consume you. That detracts from the overall quality of life." "Keep things in perspective. Life is short. So don't think [the job] is the end-all. You can always be replaced, and you can always move on and do different things."

Successful leaders show us that the experiences of adversity, properly addressed, help them dig inside and get to know themselves. That understanding becomes a base for growth. It helps them become better leaders.

Lesson 3—Know What Counts. Adversity helps leaders identify what really counts. Additionally, successful leaders learn that they must clearly express to others what really counts. "Establish a standard of values, a standard of behavior you live by. That will serve as the constant and common denominator in every decision that is forthcoming. Don't waiver on that because it provides a sense of stability. You become predictable to your people...and that's a real asset in the organization."

Your values and principles become the benchmark for actions when facing the pinch of adversity. "If you get down, you just got to again ask yourself if what you're doing is right, and then keep going." "Success is an inside game. Trust yourself. Trust where you want to go, not where others want you to go. Use your insight, gut feelings, instinct, as ways to live your life." "You've got to like what you see in the mirror. If you don't, work on it until you like it."

Successful leaders show us that the experiences of adversity, properly addressed, reveal what really counts. That awareness and the way it's communicated provide the framework for organizational action and the fiber of organization culture.

Lesson 4—You Can't Go It Alone. While adversity forces many people to reflect and turn to their inner resources, it demonstrates that "you can't go it alone." "You can't do everything yourself. You just can't. Whether it's marriage, raising children, or leading a company, you just can't do it all yourself. You have to rely on other people."

Consider this advice, again rendered from the cauldron of adversity. "Every single discipline in the business that you encounter, somebody knows more about it than you do. Go find them."

Successful leaders learn the value of strong support networks. They understand the need for these networks, at varied times, to offer emotional support, diversionary comfort, and practical advice. They learn to cultivate and deeply appreciate their support networks—family, friends, peers, faith, and spirituality.

Lesson 5—Pay Attention to People. "It's always the people. It's always about the people." Leaders understand this theme and readily espouse it. Most leaders experience their greatest sense of joy and accomplishment as well as their greatest sense of disappointment through interactions with other people.

Some of our leaders recognized that during periods of adversity—those fragile and emotional periods—the most careful attention needs to be directed toward others. "Be attentive to your people. Treat them as you want to be treated." Another, recognizing the powerful impact of others, noted simply, "Cherish your people."

Successful leaders show us that the experiences of adversity, properly addressed, help them appreciate and include others. This enhances their effectiveness to get things done and motivates those with whom they work.

Lesson 6—Become a Resource. A number of the interviewed leaders realized that facing and dealing with adversity made them far more valuable as leaders of their organizations. They had become a more informed and better-rounded resource because of the adversity they had encountered: "You know [I'm] an accumulation of all these experiences. The accumulation of all the dilemmas and the challenges, and everything they provide. [I am], in fact, a walking encyclopedia of what goes on... I think people, as a general rule, get more satisfaction out of helping and delivering than they do taking. So I think the one thing I've become is a resource. And it's nothing more than the accumulation of a lot of different experiences."

Successful leaders show us that the experiences of adversity, properly addressed, form them into powerful reservoirs of experience from which the people in the organization can draw.

Lesson 7—Hone Your Discipline. Leaders, as a group, have high levels of personal discipline. However, leaders gain and build personal discipline under the tests of adversity. Successful leaders learn that focus and discipline forge the route through adversity. Many of our leaders noted that you have to be more focused and work harder during adversity.

Successful leaders show us that the experiences of adversity, properly addressed, enhance their discipline and enable them to move with confidence through subsequent organizational battles.

Lesson 8—Maintain Credibility and Integrity. Adversity teaches leaders that they have to be true to themselves. When battling through adversity, their integrity and credibility are often on the line. "I've become a leader with greater credibility. I admit when I'm wrong." "I never go into a situation where I'm going to have to compromise my integrity."

Successful leaders show us that the experiences of adversity, properly addressed, become wonderful sparks for kindling and reinforcing leader integrity and credibility. Adversity also becomes the arena for projecting that integrity and credibility in real and powerful ways to others.

Lesson 9—There Is No Magic Bullet. Our leaders learned that the path through adversity is achieved through hard work, persistence, and consistency. Adversity is not handled through a sweeping scheme. It comes from focusing on the little things. It comes from taking a step at a time. It comes by making incremental progress. It comes from staying the course day in and day out. It comes from persevering even when you don't want to. It comes from hunkering down and doing what seems right even when you're unsure. It comes from reflecting and thinking, talking with others, adjusting, and hammering away inch by inch.

"I think one of the keys is day-to-day. You go day-to-day doing the things that need to get done. While you're going day-to-day, I keep the big picture in mind and get back to operating on principles. You really have to operate on what is right—what is the right thing to do... I don't really see where it's going to happen but I know somehow that this is going to help me. You keep doing the day to day and doing, focusing on the right things. Focus on your responsibilities, your job, whatever your responsibilities are. You really focus more, push it, focus more."

Successful leaders show us that the experience of adversity, properly approached, makes them even more focused, persistent, and steady. Faced with adversity, they learn that "you pull yourself up by the bootstraps and get to work." There is no other way. There is no magic bullet.

Lesson 10—Enjoy the Journey. Successful leaders enjoy what they do. They have passion for their work. As one executive put it, "Most of the time, even when I hate it, I like it."

Enjoyment comes from realizing that leadership is an adventure with peaks and valleys. "It's a journey. You don't really know (what will happen). Maybe I would have packed bags differently, but it was a journey. I'm always adding more to the foundation." Many of our leaders felt a need to have fun. "You've got to do all this and be able to have a lot of fun. Otherwise, it just isn't worth it."

Successful leaders show us that the experience of adversity, properly approached, makes them happier people. They look for the times of joy and the times of fun. Importantly, they relish these times. They celebrate these times. The good times become more profound precisely because they stand against the comparative check of adversity. Accordingly, successful leaders learn not to miss the opportunity to fully experience the joy.

The Wisdom of Experience

Our experiences shape us. It doesn't matter what happens to us, but what we do when something happens. Leadership is a life-long learning experience. Wisdom, if there is to be any, is derived by learning from these experiences. We found ten key lessons from our leaders' experiences of adversity.

Effective leaders manage their perceptions of the adverse event. They refuse to perceive adversity as disaster. Rather, they put the event in a larger perspective within which it becomes just another challenge and an opportunity for growth. This is an act of the will, a decision, a choice.

Leaders know themselves and know what really counts in life. Effective leaders have a code to live by as they go about resolving the obstacles before them. Furthermore, they know that no man is an island and seek support and counsel from a variety of sources.

People are paramount in the leader journey. "It's all about people" sums up what everyone had to say about their life as an executive. How people are treated during this journey was stressed over and over again. Respect and appreciation are the keys.

Leaders want to use their experiences as a source of support for others. But no matter what, dealing with adversity requires discipline, study, focus, and plain hard work if one is to go through it successfully. Yet, effective leaders know how to enjoy the journey no matter how rugged it is. They introduce fun and humor into the entire process.

As we have emphasized, adversity brings out the character of the leader for better or for worse. Living according to principles of integrity and credibility makes a better person, no matter the outcome; virtue is indeed its own reward. Perseverance under duress is what strengthens character for the inevitable life events that lie before us.

20

The Rebound Culture

"If you don't misstep, you're not stepping."

The company had been the darling of the high tech industry. Highflying stock and unprecedented returns made Cisco Systems one of the true power players. But all that toppled in the first quarter of 2001. Revenues were down a dramatic 30 percent from the previous quarter and 8,500 layoffs were announced. The stock plummeted. If that wasn't enough, its vice president of business development was named in an FBI affidavit. Things could hardly be worse.

Enter John Chambers, the company's pioneering CEO. Chambers is upbeat and encouraging. He even argues that the woes of the tech sector may play to Cisco's favor in the long run. He argues that Cisco's rapid acquisition route for growth will gain new momentum as strapped companies, hungry for capital, can be acquired at bargain rates. Business Week described him as "stubbornly optimistic." Chambers goes even further to express his confidence in the business and its future. He decided to reduce his annual salary from $157 million to one dollar.[1]

A New World

We are convinced that today's leader must practice the leader rebound in order to survive and succeed. Yet the responsibilities of leadership call for more. Today's leaders must bring the rebound spirit to their organizations. Leaders must build a rebound culture that is real, alive, and operating on a day-to-day basis.

The demands for rebound have never been greater. A quick purview of recent business history tells us clearly that no organization can escape adversity and crisis. Consistent blue-chip winners are not immune—ask IBM. The new power elite are not immune—ask Cisco Systems. Some are fighting to survive their own mistakes and misreadings—ask Xerox. Others are battling across a landscape laced with both unbridled opportunities and destructive landmines—ask Microsoft. Competition intensifies and the market is unrelenting. All organizations must rebound quickly. Their rebound strategies will spell the difference between success and failure.

Beyond strategy, there is a personal need for rebound in every organization. The people are the ones torn and stressed by the ravages of business adversity. Business adversity brings fear. Will jobs be lost? Will I survive? Will career progress be put on hold? Will working at this place stop being fun? Will this tension that seems to grip me as soon as I walk in the door ever go away? The need to rebound from these fears and concerns tugs at the masses.

Organization culture is, at times, a fuzzy notion. It is one of those concepts we recognize but have difficulty explaining. Culture retains its mystery because it is unwritten. Yet, its impact is deep and sweeping. Individual behaviors and practices are often guided and defined by our culture. As one leader stated, "We do it that way here because it's part of our culture." The need for cultural affinity even drives our strategy as exemplified by the statement, "that move would be out of sync with our culture."

Let's offer a basic definition: Culture is a set of key values and expectations that are commonly shared and accepted by the members of an organization. Although generally unwritten, culture is a powerful presence. It defines the values and expectations of the organization. Culture tells members of the organization what to believe in, how to do things, and what is, or isn't, appropriate. People understand that these are the values and expectations that count and adhering to them will bring rewards and success.

Building Culture

Much has been written on how organizational culture develops. Culture evolves and emerges but it can be managed, directed, and changed. While change is possible, it does not happen overnight.

Over the last 15 years, we have worked with a number of organizations that have consciously changed their corporate cultures. Most often, these businesses shifted from a strongly centralized, command-and-control culture to one that emphasized involvement, collaboration, openness, and teamwork. Management implemented a series of interlocking steps and practices to encourage this shift. While the changes rarely came smoothly, they came. They came as the new values and expectations were repeatedly clarified. Changes came when the values were consistently discussed and reinforced through day-to-day activity.

A rebound culture projects two fundamental themes. First, a rebound culture says that mistakes, adversity, and even crisis will come. But it also conveys a second theme: these adversities will be overcome through persistence, adherence to principles, and organizational support. Importantly, a rebound culture does not develop from idle words, and it is not a pep talk. It is developed by injecting the idea of rebound into the very fiber of the organization. It is a spirit and a philosophy. The people of the organization hear it, know it, believe it, and see it practiced over and over again.

This rebound culture is not new. We've seen evidence of it for years. Recall the classic story about IBM founder Tom Watson's encounter with a young manager who faced a crisis. Misreading a risky venture, the manager's mistake had cost the company over $10 million. Certain of his impending termination, the young manager nervously addressed Watson. "I guess you want my resignation." Watson's response has become part of the folklore of IBM. "You can't be serious. We've just spent $10 million educating you."[2]

This story illustrates how the decisions and actions of an organization's leaders can form a culture. These types of stories are repeated over and over again. They become living examples of the rebound culture. Then they become more than just stories; they become the norm, the expectation. People believe that this is how the company actually operates. Accordingly, a culture is defined.

The Leader Reinforces the Culture

Rebound organizations are led by rebound leaders. The leader is always on center stage. Others can easily determine what values and actions their leaders hold dear. They then emulate those values and actions. This wins favor and demonstrates organizational loyalty. Employees presume it to be the way to secure rewards and advancement.

There is a fundamental truth to organizational life. People do what they are rewarded for doing. Leaders must be sure that their rebound culture is reinforced and reinforced consistently.

The rebound culture is reinforced through the leader's attitude and actions. People are always looking and asking, "Does the leader believe in and practice the rebound?"

The rebound culture is reinforced through the speeches and other forms of communication the leader makes. The rebound culture is reinforced when those exhibiting rebound characteristics are recognized and promoted within the organization. The rebound culture is reinforced when the business commits its time, energy, and resources to ensuring that becoming a rebound company is a top priority.

Any single one of these pieces, in isolation, may not make a major cultural difference. All of these pieces, collectively, provide a consistent picture that drives the logic and the merit of rebound throughout the organization. In this way, the value of rebound becomes deep and pervasive. It becomes the prevailing culture.

There are few secrets in most organizations. Leaders are only able to hide adversity from their people for a short period of time. Generally, coworkers have worked with the leader long enough to know that something is up. They read the signs.

The rebound leader must make some tough decisions: How much of the adversity do I share with my people? How much of it do I keep from my people? When is the proper time to share? Part of that answer depends on the nature of the adversity and part of it depends on the nature of the leader. However, we uncovered some general guidelines.

1. Communication. The way a leader communicates during adversity affects the organization and its people. Communications also express the rebound culture.

Sooner or later, the basics of major adversities have to be shared. This is particularly true in the business arena, whether the adversity is a major mistake or a full-blown crisis. Often, leaders share because they have no other recourse. Those in the organization might not know exactly what is happening, but they are aware that something is up. One leader noted, "My people can read me like a book. They will sense something is wrong. If I don't fill in the blanks, they do, and rumors start."

Most leaders shared the issue with their team after they had sorted out the nature and extent of the adversity. The top executive team is generally the first group to learn the situation. Together, the leader with the rest of the executive team reviews the pieces, defines the issues, and figure out a plan. Then, the plan is communicated to the rest of the organization.

This communication to the masses is quite important. The leadership team should have a plan in place before speaking in detail to the people of the organization. Leaders need not define all the details and specifics, but, at the least, a broad, general plan should be provided. Most people like to be involved, and they want to help. However, most people do not want the responsibility of sifting and digging to the root of the crisis. That's what they expect leaders to do. In fact, most research suggests that people want leaders who are decisive when it comes to dealing with severe adversity or crisis.

2. Training. Leaders build and reinforce the culture of an organization through training efforts. Orientation training solidifies the company's values, expectations, and approaches for the company's newest employees. Ongoing training emphasizes what the company values and stresses. Some companies, like Edward Jones, require and support continuing education. They make an obvious statement about growth and innovation and how it is maintained.

Companies that believe in the rebound philosophy should provide rebound training. For the past two years, we have worked with two large business clients on helping their people deal with the massive changes affecting their industry and their business. Call it what they want, it is rebound training. We talk about understanding the inevitable ups and downs. We help their managers recognize what they can and cannot control. We encourage their leaders to find creative ways to deal with what they can affect. We

187

help them develop and practice methods and patterns for dealing with the trauma they feel. These companies believe in rebound. They espouse it openly. But, more importantly, they invest in training to increase the capacity for rebound throughout their business.

3. Crisis and Deviations. For many people, culture is really defined during crisis. In other words, it's in the tough times that real values shine forth.

We noted this theme earlier in the book. It is important. Leaders can say anything they want. But what do they practice? How do they act when the pressure is on? Some leaders talk the rebound game, yet display little resilience in the face of crisis. The organization's people get a mixed message. On one hand, the leader says, "Hang in there. Stay the course." On the other hand, the leader "flies mad" when adversity strikes. In the process, the rebound culture is undermined. Leaders will either reinforce or undermine the rebound culture by how they handle organizational crises. Everybody is watching and anticipating.

Think about the following scenarios, fresh from the daily business headlines. Faced with disappointing revenues, mixed financial expectations, and slipping market confidence, many large firms have made massive layoffs affecting thousands of workers. Admittedly, these cost-cutting moves may help shore-up the firm's stock performance. Against this downsizing backdrop, a few bold businesses have decided to act differently. These firms have held the line and made alternate moves to address cost issues. Salaries have been cut. Discretionary spending has been eliminated. While these moves have been trying and painful, the people of the business, for the most part, have been retained.

Consider the differing cultural messages. On one hand, the response to crisis is a sweeping elimination of people. On the other hand, it is a series of sweeping moves intended to do everything possible to keep from eliminating people. These latter firms display a different approach to adversity than the quick fix of downsizing. Their approach speaks of hard work, dedication, persistence, and the commitment to stay the course. They take the broad view. A culture that values loyalty over expediency is born.

4. Image and Honesty. In the midst of adversity, most leaders feel the need to project a positive image to the people of their organization. This is particularly important during the early stages of adversity when disillusionment is present and deep reflection is taking place. The cultural tone of rebound needs to be set.

Even when leaders experience that evasive fear of failure, they have to be careful not to let the emotions of fear run through the organization. One leader spoke of the early days of a trying crisis: "I come to grips with the realities. There is fear here. But I can't come across as [projecting] fear." Another said, "When I get down, I often show it. I try not to display that I'm down." He went on to say he needed some time to "lift himself up" before facing his people.

One leader said, "You create your own atmosphere. If you allow yourself to be negative, it will suck you in and suck you down." Another leader made a nearly identical comment. "I try to be in an up mood. If I'm not, I can drag others down." We all understand and have experienced these emotions. The people in the business pick up on the mood and tone that the leader sets. In turn, that mood affects their thinking and performance.

This image creates a bit of a dilemma. We certainly do not suggest dishonesty, and we cannot condone deception. In the throes of adversity, leaders are often hurting. Internally, they are far from being cool, calm, and collected. However, they realize it is not best to share pain, uncertainty, and disillusionment with the people in their organizations. Leaders need time to sort things through. They will share, but that comes later. So leaders put on "their game face." They try to project the rebound before they even experience it. One seasoned leader looked over a successful career, but one with its fair share of controversy and adversity. "When I'm down, I try to project an image different from that… You have the ability to be a good actor when you are down."

Rebound leaders project the leader rebound before they fully experience it. They tell their people that things will work out. Some of those hearing it probably don't even believe it. But that's not important. The key is that the leader is saying it. The positive mask actually helps the leader's personal rebound. Think about what occurs. A confident image helps manage personal perceptions of adversity. The open expression of confidence actually helps the leader avoid languishing in adversity and sends a psychological signal to the leader that things will work out.

Is this dishonest? No, the leader is not lying. The leader is not saying the company will survive while knowing that all evidence points to the contrary. The leader is not promising business as usual while knowing that drastic changes loom on the horizon. Rather, the leader is presenting an image of confidence. Whatever storms may come, the business and its people will emerge. Different? Yes. Battered? In all likelihood. But, they will emerge.

We recently worked with a strong rebound leader whose business faced a series of rocky trials. He boldly called his people together in groups of 25 to 30. He listened to their concerns. He told them what he knew about the trials facing the business, and he was honest about what he did not know. He spoke of options and contingencies. He told them what he thought would happen and why. Yet, he was clear that there were no guarantees.

His message was clear. "We've been through these kinds of things before. There may have been different issues, but we've seen it before. We survived. You remember. We'll do it again." He played on the adversity memory of those in his audience. He showed them, in ways they could recall and understand, that rebound was part of his leadership and part of their shared experience in the business. He sold the rebound image, and he reinforced the rebound culture.

This was not dishonest because the leader actually believed it. He believed it because it was part of his past. Even though he hadn't experienced it yet in this situation (and neither had others), the framework for rebound was established.

The Future

We hope that leaders will sense the importance of the rebound on both a personal and a broader organizational level. We hope that leaders will discover the steps of rebound and begin to translate these steps into reality for their businesses.

The leader rebound can be developed. Similarly, the rebound culture can be built. We encourage leaders to take the tough, demanding steps necessary to rebound. Further, we encourage them to incorporate those steps into their leadership approach and style. And critically, we encourage leaders to take this rebound philosophy to their businesses and use it as a practical operational philosophy.

Let's end with the words of those leaders we interviewed: "Whatever circumstance or situation you are in, make yourself into that kind of boss who ... strives on... continues on... finds out what it takes... You end up being successful..." "It's not because I'm brilliant...It's because I've been through it." "I have always seen that glass that is 50 percent liquid as half full. I even have trouble envisioning it as half empty. I guess I may be naïve, but I sleep extremely well." "Develop and think about tests, rules, morals, and principles... Always take the test. Try to turn problems into opportunities."

"Nothing magical, but it seems to work!"

The Wisdom of Experience

The world is marked by uncertainty and this is no less true for the world of business. Adversity is a fact of life and no organization escapes adversity and crisis. This is why a rebound culture is critical.

Organizational culture is a kind of unwritten prescription of how people should think and act. And the organization's top executives drive the culture by their words and deeds. Here, then, are the essential elements of a rebound culture: Everyone needs to know that adversity is part and parcel of any business, as well as life itself. Perseverance is required and with it the organization will win. And to get successfully through any adverse advent, people need to depend upon one another for support, encouragement, cooperation, and recognition. These organizational habits have to be in place before adversity strikes.

The leader models the process. The CEO sets the tone and influences the organization's leader-follower chain. If the CEO is savage, so are the followers. If the CEO adheres to a set of principles, so will the followers.

Leader must form a plan of action and then tell the truth. In the emergency room, everyone expects the ER doctor to take action rather than sit there sharing how he feels about the bloody mess he sees. So, too, it must be with the organization's leaders. Their goal is not to panic their employees, but to encourage them in the rebound process by setting a course of action and exhibiting an air of confidence based in their personal commitment and will to succeed.

Appendix

The Nature of the Leader Rebound Study

We used an interview methodology to research *The Adversity Challenge*. Researchers commonly use the interview design to gain perspectives from front-line leaders. Prior works prompted our thinking, offered direction, and suggested themes and insights. These studies are representative of many powerful insights revealed through leader interviews. Collectively, these works have contributed to our understanding of leadership and the requirements for leadership effectiveness. For instance, in a classic study, Bennis and Nanus used an informal and unstructured format to interview 60 CEOs. Their interviews addressed the keys to effective leadership.[1] The editors of *Harvard Business Review* interviewed 16 prominent leaders from business and political arenas and explored the values and behaviors of successful leaders.[2] Using the interview format, Dauphinais and Price presented ideas on improving corporate performance from 34 CEOs throughout the world.[3] Leslie and VanVelsor interviewed 20 senior executives to compare successful and derailed managers. They found that successful managers were able to adapt, establish strong collaborative relationships, and were exceptionally intelligent.[4] Neff and Citron, in profiles and interviews with 50 of America's top business leaders, uncovered 10 traits for success. Among these were inner peace and a positive attitude.[5]

While these works provided a framework for us, our study was different. It concentrated on the nature of the leader experience. It emphasized a multi-faceted look at leadership by exploring the interplay of career and other dimensions of the leader's life (such as family, friends, community, and spirituality). Considerable emphasis was given to success, its meaning, and how it was attained.

Method and Analysis

We contacted prospective leader participants. A brief overview of the study and its purpose—to provide insights into the life of the leader that could be translated to help others—was presented. This was followed by a request for leader participation. Appointments for personal interviews were set, and these interviews took place at the executives' offices. All participants were senior executives being in either the top or one of the top leader positions in their respective companies. Most of the participants, in addition to their organizational identities, had held key community and service positions of leadership. All participants had been recognized by various business bodies for their achievements.

The interviews followed a structured questionnaire format. Open-ended questions were used, and follow-up probes were added as needed. We conducted all interviews. All interviews were recorded and transcribed for analysis.

Two rounds of interviews took place. In the first round, 30 leaders participated. These interviews ranged from 60 minutes to slightly over two hours, with the average duration being about 85 minutes. After the initial analysis of these interviews, eight additional interviews were conducted. These follow-up interviews were conducted to gain more depth and clarity around certain issues and themes. These interviews were shorter, most lasting about one hour. A total of 35 leaders participated in the study.

We then conducted a content analysis of these transcripts.[6] We coded the responses according to general concepts and grouped them into generalized themes. Themes were organized into a concept map from which the basic structure of *The Adversity Challenge* was drawn.

Notes

Chapter 1

1. Norman Brinker and Donald T. Phillips. *On the Brink.*
Arlington, TX: The Summit Publishing Group, 1996, p. 181.

Chapter 2

1. There are some excellent recent works on the role and responsibility of leadership that have helped shaped our thinking. For example see:

John P. Kotter. *John P. Kotter on What Leaders Really Do.* Boston: Harvard
Business School Press, 1999;

Colin Price and G. William Dauphinais (eds). *Straight from the CEO: The
World's Top Business Leaders Reveal Ideas that Every Manager Can Use.* New
York: Simon & Schuster Trade, 1999;

Thomas J. Neff and James M. Citron. *Lessons from the Top: The Search for
America's Best Business Leaders.* New York: Currency and Doubleday,
1999.

2. Henry Mintzberg. *The Nature of Managerial Work.* New York: Harper & Row,
1973.

Chapter 3

1. See for example, the classic work:

J. R. Hackman and G. R. Oldham. *Work Redesign.* Reading, MA: Addison-
Wesley, 1980.

Chapter 5

1. This parallels previous studies:

Russ S. Moxley. "Hardships." In Cynthia D. McCauley, Russ D. Moxley, and
Ellen Van Velsor (eds). *The CCL Handbook of Leadership Development.* San
Francisco: Jossey-Bass, 1998;

Morgan W. McCall Jr., Michael M. Lombardo, and Ellen Van Velsor. *The
Lessons of Experience: How Successful Executives Develop on the Job.*
Lexington, MA: Lexington Books, 1988.

2. Jean B. Leslie and Ellen Van Velsor. *A Look at Derailment Today.* Greensboro,
North Carolina: Center for Creative Leadership, 1996.

3. Michael Eisner and Tony Schwartz. *Work in Progress: Risking Failure,
Surviving Success.* New York: Hyperion, 1999.

Chapter 6

1. An excellent recent review is offered by the book, *Harvard Business Review on
Change.* Boston: Harvard Business School Press, 1998.

2. The original work was Leon Festinger. *A Theory of Cognitive Dissonance.* New
York: Harper, 1957.

Chapter 7

1. John P. Kotter. *Leading Change*. Boston: Harvard Business School Publishing, 1996.
2. McCall, et al., p. 87.

Chapter 8

1. See for example, Bernard M. Bass. *Handbook of Leadership: A Survey of Theory and Research*. New York: Free Press, 1990
   A. Howard and D. W. Bray. *Managerial Lives in Transition: Advancing Age and Changing Times*. New York: Guilford Press, 1988.
2. See the classic work of Rotter. Julian B. Rotter. "Generalized Expectancies for Internal versus External Control of Reinforcement." *Psychological Monographs*, 80, 609, 1966.
   D. Miller; M.F.R. Kets de Vries, and J. Toulouse. "Locus of Control and Its Relationship to Strategy, Environment, and Structure." *Academy of Management Journal*, 25, 237-253, 1982.
3. This form of coping is similar to that identified by Maddi and Kobasa as transformational coping.
   Salvatore R. Maddi and Suzanne C. Kobasa. *The Hardy Executive: Health Under Stress*. Homewood, IL: Dow Jones-Irwin, 1984.
4. See some original work in this area such as:
   R. D. Kaplan. "Social Support, Person-Environment Fit and Coping." In L. Ferman and J. Gordin (eds.), *Mental Health and the Economy*. Kalamazoo, MI: Upjohn Foundation, 1979
   S. Cobb. "Social Support as a Moderator of Life Stress." *Psychosomatic Medicine*, 38, 300-314, 1976.
5. See Maddi and Kobasa, 1984.
6. Maddi and Kobasa, 1984.
7. R. L. Payne; P.B. Warr and J. Hartley. "Social Class and Psychological Ill-Health During Unemployment." *Sociology of Health and Illness*, 6, 152-174, 1984.
8. Laura L. Nash. *Believers in Business*. Nashville: Thomas Nelson, 1994.
9. Edwin A. Locke. *The Essence of Leadership: The Four Keys to Leading Effectively*. San Francisco: Jossey-Bass, 1991.
   John P. Kotter. *John P. Kotter on What Leaders Really Do*. Boston: Harvard Business School Publishing, 1999.

Chapter 10

1. Jeanie Daniel Duck. "Managing Change: The Art of Balancing." In *Harvard Business Review on Change*. Boston: Harvard Business School Press, 1998, pp. 67-69.

Chapter 11

1. "A Conversation with Servant-Leader and Author James Autry." *The Servant Leader*. Winter, 2001, 1-3.
2. An excellent overview is provided by Richard W. Woodman, John E. Sawyer, and Ricky W. Griffin. "Toward a Theory of Organizational Creativity." *The Academy of Management Review*, 18, 2, April, 1993, 293-321.

3.   See Robert E. Quinn, Sue R. Faerman, Michael P. Thompson, and Michael R. McGrath. *Becoming a Master Manager: A Competency Framework*. 4th ed. New York: John Wiley, 1996, pp. 348-349.
4.   Roger Kelley. *Letters to My Children*. 1999.

Chapter 12

1.   Delores Ambrose. *Leadership: The Journey Inward*. Dubuque, Iowa: Kendall/Hunt Publishing, 1991, p. 38.
2.   This example is taken from Ken Melrose's essay. Ken Melrose. "Putting Servant-Leadership Into Practice." In Larry C. Spears (ed.). *Insights on Leadership.* New York: John Wiley and Sons, 1998, 279-281.
3.   Melrose, 1998.
4.   This example is taken from Thomas Melville. "Surviving the Spotlight." *Success*. February/March, 2001.

Chapter 13

1.   John F. Welsh. "Timeless Principles." *Executive Excellence*. 18, 2 ,February, 2001, 3-4.
2.   Melba Newsome. "All Pro Construction." *Success*. November, 2000.
3.   Bethany McClean. "Taking on Prostate Cancer, Andy Grove." *Fortune*. May 13, 1996.

Chapter 14

1.   Robert Langreth. "Refusing to Die." *Forbes*. April 16, 2001, 368-371.
2.   See the excellent work of Paul G. Stoltz. *Adversity Quotient*. New York: John Wiley and Sons, 1997.
     Maddi and Kobasa, *The Hardy Executive: Health Under Stress*, 1984.

Chapter 15

1.   Jill Brooke. "Grief and Greatness." *Forbes*. April 16, 2001, 182-186.
2.   Everett Alvarez Jr. with Samuel Schreiner. *Code of Conduct*. New Yrok: Donald I. Fine, 1991.
3.   Everett Alnarez Jr. and Anthony Pitch. *Chained Eagle*. New York: Donald I. Fine, 1989.

Chapter 16

1.   Michael S. Malone. "Been Here, Done This." *Forbes* ASAP. May 28, 2001, 47-50.
2.   Ibid., 48.

Chapter 17

1.   Gordon Bethune and Scott Huler. *From Worst to First*. New York: John Wiley and Sons, 1998, p. 11.

Chapter 18

1.   Edgar H. Schein. *Organization Culture and Leadership*. San Francisco: Jossey-Bass, 1996.

Chapter 20

1. Peter Elstrom. "Sorry Cisco. The Old Answers Won't Work." *Business Week.* April 30, 2001, 39
    "Report: Cisco CEO Cuts Pay." http://cnnfn.companies (accessed 5-15-2001).
2. From Bennis and Nanus, 1985, p. 76.

Appendix

1. Warren Bennis and Burt Nanus. *Leaders: Strategies for Taking Charge.* New York: Harper & Row, 1985.
2. *Harvard Business Review Interviews with CEOs.* Boston: Harvard Business School Press, 2000.
3. Colin Price and G. William Dauphinais (eds). *Straight from the CEO: The World's Top Business Leaders Reveal Ideas that Every Manager Can Use.* New York: Simon & Schuster Trade, 1999.
4. Jean B. Leslie and Ellen Van Velsor. *Cross-National Comparison of Effective Leadership and Teamwork toward a Global Workforce.* Center for Creative Leadership, 1998.
5. Thomas J. Neff and James M. Citron. *Lessons from the Top: The Search for America's Best Business Leaders.* New York: Currency and Doubleday, 1999.
6. See, for example, Amanda Coffey and Paul Atkinson. *Making Sense of Qualitative Data: Complementary Research Strategies.* Thousand Oaks, CA: Sage Publications, 1996
    Anselm Strauss and Juliet Corbin. *Basics of Qualitative Research: Techniques and Procedures for Developing Grounded Theory.* (2nd ed.). Thousand Oaks, CA: Sage Publications, 1998.

About the Authors

Charles R. (Chuck) Stoner, D.B.A., is McCord Professor of Executive Management Development and Professor of Business Management at Bradley University. Dr. Stoner received both his M.B.A. and doctorate from Florida State University. He has authored or co-authored four textbooks, and his research has yielded over 50 refereed articles and papers. He is co-author of the popular introductory text *Business: An Integrative Approach* (Irwin/McGraw-Hill). Specializing in leadership and organizational change, Dr. Stoner is an active consultant and popular speaker. He has worked with the Leadership Development Center since its inception in 1985.

Foster College of Business, Bradley University
Peoria, IL 61625
309-677-2311
crs@bradley.edu

John F. (Jack) Gilligan, Ph.D., is president and chief executive officer of Fayette Companies. He received his Ph.D. from the University of Idaho and completed a post-doctoral fellowship in clinical psychology from University of Illinois School of Medicine.

He is chairman of the Peoria, Illinois Workforce Development Board, vice-president of the Employers' Association of Illinois board of directors, a member of the Multi-Ad, Inc. board of directors, and a board member of the Drug Prevention Network of the Americas. Dr. Gilligan has provided managerial training and consultation to managers of Fortune 500 corporations as well as to international organizations.

Fayette Companies, 600 Fayette Ave.
Peoria, IL 61603
309-671-8005

OTHER BOOKS BY EXECUTIVE EXCELLENCE